DOWN
THERE

BOOKS PUBLISHED

DOWN

Jose Yglesias

NEW YORK AND CLEVELAND

THERE

THE WORLD PUBLISHING COMPANY

Published by The World Publishing Company
2231 West 110th Street, Cleveland, Ohio 44102
Published simultaneously in Canada by
Nelson, Foster & Scott Ltd.

First Printing—1970

Library of Congress Catalog Card Number: 76-128483
Printed in the United States of America

WORLD PUBLISHING
TIMES MIRROR

For Marysa Navarro Gerassi

CONTENTS

DOWN THERE

I

Latin America
on My Mind

I leave each Latin American country as if I have lost the battle to remain myself. No matter how short the visit—and the chapters in this book on Brazil, Chile, and Peru were the result of ten-day stays—I have given way, the moment I step off the plane, to the sounds of my first language, learned, of all places, in the South of the United States, the Latin section of Tampa, Florida. To speak a language is to adopt a cultural manner, a way of seeing and doing, that has formed it. In countries where Spanish is spoken, it becomes difficult for me to act like an observer, and impossible to pretend to objectivity. In 1960, a Cuban poet said angrily to me, "It is

simply a geographical accident that you were born up there
—don't deny you are one of us!" Only when I get on the
plane again can I recover the feeling that I am a Yankee,
and begin to put that distance between myself and the
experience I have undergone that is necessary for writing.
For it is only in the writing, by once more coming close to
what you have lived through, that you can resolve these con-
flicts. Life doesn't let you: on the next trip it happens again.

This is, without question, a rather subjective way to approach so large a chunk of geography as Latin America, but
the writers who have taught me something about the countries they have visited have never hidden behind the impersonal "we." George Borrow on Spain, Frances Calderon de
la Barca on Mexico, Richard Henry Dana on Cuba, Susan
Sontag on Hanoi took me there with them in a way that no
professional journalist ever did. I prefer the snapshots and
anecdotes of someone just returned from a two-week pack-
age tour of all the capitals of Europe to one of those special
sections *The New York Times* publishes every January pur-
porting to give you a socio-politico-economic roundup of the
continent, not only because the former is likely to be livelier
and more vivid but because it does not lend itself so con-
veniently to lying.

The moment a reporter removes himself from the scene
he is describing, he makes it easier for himself to lie. He
need not tell you which event he read about and which he
saw for himself; he does not, as scholars say, distinguish between primary and secondary sources; and the reader cannot
help but credit the reporter with an equal knowledge of all
the things he writes. I am not, of course, speaking about
vulgar fabrication—no style is impervious to that—but
about the distortion that occurs, and is hidden from the
reader, when a social or political scene is described without

reference to the person who is describing it. In life this cannot happen. When you listen to someone, you judge not only on the basis of his statements but of what you know or can guess about him; the printed word has, however, a kind of authority that makes you forget someone as full of prejudices as you and I has written it.

Objectivity. It does not exist. No one can turn into a blank, and everyone is out to win you to his point of view. The writer who does not try is a bore, and the attempt to be objective is suspect, for it is seldom sincere and often disingenuous. It is the cutting edge of our prejudices and sympathies that opens up any subject in a way that nothing else can. To have tried to shuck my personal background and sympathies while in Latin America would have been foolish. I might as well not have spoken Spanish, and viewed with ignorant impartiality all the citizens of those countries as "natives," as do many corporation businessmen stationed overseas. I think of them as my brothers—no other word will do—as people I knew quite well in that Latin colony where I grew up in Florida. I say this not only to put my cards on the table but also to help explain, in this personal way, the mentality of present-day Latin Americans.

When I was young, there were some forty thousand Latins living in Tampa, most of them in a section known as Ybor City and most working in the cigar industry. They were highly organized in everything they did, in their own trade unions, mutual aid societies, cultural centers, cooperative grocery stores, and they spoke one language, Spanish; but they lived, as a community, within the structure of American society and had no political or economic power. Needless to say, Ybor City was not a nation, as are the countries of Latin America; but the simultaneous drives by the larger American society of assimilation and rejection—ideally, we were all Americans; in practice, "Cuban niggers"—created a psychology among us in Ybor City that I recognize in Latin America, the psychology of the colonized.

This is the psychology of people who have been wounded in their very souls. Most Americans believe that the economic activities of American corporations in Latin America —or in any part of the world, for that matter—are job-creating, modernizing endeavors of an almost altruistic nature; that the politics of our international diplomacy means to create, through organizations such as the O.A.S., an independent collective voice for Latin America in world councils; that even our occasional military interventions down there, with their selfless expenditure of American lives, are in the interest of stability and democracy for Latin Americans. Most Latin Americans know this to be untrue. Raw materials and profits are the magnet that draws American companies; diplomacy, the means whereby these activities are legitimized; military intervention, the trump card of our diplomacy. Some know this in just such politico-economic abstract terms, others in the unending poverty of their lives; all, hurt in their national honor, blame us.

The elders in my hometown, even when born in Florida, resisted the encroachment of American ways. Partly because what one is born to is more comfortable, more sensible— you don't change national identity easily. Partly because they feared that the greater individual freedom for young people, especially girls, that the American ambience encouraged would change our morality and challenge the lines of authority of Spanish family relationships. Yet they might have felt less animosity toward American mores—been less scornful of "those barbarians with hair on their teeth"—if the immediate American environment had been appreciative of some of the extraordinary achievements of the Latin community. The two hospitals built by the cigarmakers' mutual aid societies were, when I was a boy, the two best in Tampa. The societies had also built four fine social centers; they contained theaters, ball rooms, cafes, gymnasiums, and small libraries, and they encouraged amateur theatricals which were well attended. First-rate theatrical companies from Spain and Mexico and Cuba came to Ybor City, and many great concert performers. In the factories, the hiring of readers was an innovation of Tampa cigarmakers that spread to other parts of the world, a technique in adult liberal arts education on the job yet to be bettered; the workers set up their own committees in each factory and paid with weekly contributions for the reader they selected in auditions followed by voting; for four hours each day they listened to newspapers and magazines being read to them and to a novel that they themselves chose, again by vote. The American Medical Association fought the societies' medical plan by not allowing its members to serve on the societies' staff of doctors or to practice in their hospitals. The cigar manufacturers arbitrarily ended the institution of readers during the Depression, and the American community supported the manufacturers, as always, when the cigarmakers went on strike to regain their readers. The cigarmakers were class-conscious trade unionists, as were many American workers, and that they were met with coercion and violence, as were other American workers, had nothing to do with the national culture of the cigarmakers. Their unionism, too, was rejected as a foreign ideology that should have been left on other shores. Is it any wonder that to those oldtimers in Ybor City the mentality of the Ku Klux Klan—the KKK that at rifle point broke up their meetings at the Labor Temple, built also with the workers' contributions—represents America?

In Ybor City we had the option of claiming we were Americans. In a sense, it could be said to us that if we did not like it here we should go back where we came from. We were offered, for better or for worse, American citizenship, and were told, as we went to schools outside the community, that we were as good as anyone else. We knew that all along; our problem was trusting that sufficient other Americans did. Becoming American was a personal struggle, and whatever scars we bear, some of us arrived. Obviously, no such solution exists for Latin Americans—except for Cuban exiles—and to suggest it would seem to most of them the final solution. They have no alternative but to reject our presence and our influence, and the forms of this rejection are what underlies my accounts in this book of visits to four Latin American countries.

These trips were undertaken as assignments by the Sunday Magazine of *The New York Times*, and when discussing what might be the themes of the articles I would write for them, one editor closed the discussion by saying that whatever I chose could not help but be a contribution. "We know so little about the countries down there," he said. I was disposed to agree with him that week, for I had just heard from a friend of his experience with one of our important journals, a magazine that I had thought would publish my friend's article on the Tupamaros, the urban guerrillas of Uruguay. My friend reached the editor-in-chief on the phone and asked if he would be interested in an article on Montevideo and did not mention the Tupamaros. The editor replied that indeed he would be interested, and just before he hung up asked, "Tell me, where is Montevideo?"

This would not have happened if Montevideo was the

capital of a small European country, and Latin American-ists are always making the point that we know very little about Latin America. It is true, but we Americans have the habit of berating ourselves for our shortcomings; the citizens of developed European countries are as uninformed about Latin America as we are, but it is not a public issue with them. In the last twenty years our college and university presses have begun to pay close attention, and our trade publishers have introduced us to most of their important writers; anyone familiar with the publishing industry knows how carefully any new book by a Latin American is considered for publication here. We have inherited an apathy to the literature of the Spanish language that is due to our traditional ties to the mainstream of cultural and political developments in Western Europe, and one result is that most of the great Spanish writers have yet to be translated and published in our country. This lack of interest in Spanish culture is an historically reinforced trait with which it is difficult to argue, based, as it is, on Spain's role in the Counter-Reformation. Our cultural estrangement carried over to Latin America, and a century's involvement with that continent, greater in some ways than with Europe, has not changed our attitude. That it has not also reflects, I think, guilt about our relationship to the Latin Americans and a need to continue to believe that the culture of those we mistreat is inferior to ours.

Much of the indifference is beginning to be a matter of the past. An incident more significant than that of the American editor who did not know where to place Montevideo is that of a Latin American historian who told me he was unwilling to learn English well. He is at ease with French, Italian, Portuguese, and knows enough English to keep up with publications in his field. Yet he would not want to improve it, in order not to be tempted, he confessed, by offers from the United States. The number of important scholars lured away by American universities, he said, is so great as to constitute an intellectual drain harmful to Latin America. "Curiously, they do not balk even at radicals," he added. "No sooner does one of our intellectuals get into trouble with one of our unfortunate governments than some American foundation or university bails him out with a job in your country." He believes that this is a policy, and an imperialist one, aimed at neutralizing and bringing into our fold the natural leaders of an independent Latin America—a charge the Cubans also made in 1966 when so many left-wing South American intellectuals showed up in New York for the P.E.N. International Congress—but however one characterizes this, it is certainly not evidence of lack of interest.

Our newspapers compare favorably with those of non-South American countries in reporting news events. With the exception of *Le Monde*, there is probably no newspaper that equals in its coverage of Latin America that great fact collector, *The New York Times*, although in this area it is not as thorough as with Europe. Despite our State Department's attempts to isolate us from Cuba—so extreme that it has amounted, in the words of an American publisher, to self-censorship—our newspapers and magazines have managed to publish a considerable number of reports. Better ones in the main than what I have seen in English journals. Yet we are right to be restive about what one finds currently, not in special studies and university press books but in the papers and magazines available to the general public. Restive if only because almost every major news event comes as a surprise. Urban guerrillas break out in Uruguay—but wasn't it a well-ordered, constitutional democracy? The Peruvian generals nationalize American-owned companies—but weren't these men in our back pocket?

I think there are two reasons why we are unhappy. First, our knowledge of South America is not equal to the role we play there. We are the dominant influence in that continent, we all know, even if we are not all willing to learn the reason for this; and if we are to be big brother, general counsel, and generous lender, we should be better informed than other nations. Second, as the surprising turns of events there indicate, the quality of the information we get cannot be the best. Perhaps there is a third reason. The confident way our diplomats and generals have gone about the world fighting communism has led us into the disaster of Viet Nam, and that may be making many of us feel that our confidence has everywhere been misplaced.

For me only the second reason seems valid. At least as a fruitful subject for discussion. There is something wrong with the information we are getting. Obviously, reporting facts is not enough. And there are certain facts that are not reported; what people think is one of them. An editor of the *Times* took a look at my report on Chile and said, "He says it's a democracy—why all the talk about revolution?" It unsteadies my mind to think about that response—where does one begin to explain?

Does one start with the facts of underdevelopment and give a précis of the economists who have told us that only economic planning can make development possible? But I am not sufficiently qualified to be convincing in this field —the subject alone of how to attain the necessary capital accumulation for industrialization of a capitalist or socialist economy leads to enormous argumentation—and in any case, such an explanation is only a beginning. It barely leads us to the question of revolutions; it does not tell us why they are necessary in the third world. If this economic planning is to be socialist, I might explain, then there is political and economic power to be relinquished by the national ruling classes—and by U.S. firms and banks. Even when the changes are only reforms in some sectors of the economy, as in Peru, government intervention against particular economic groups sets up a heightened class struggle that to some means revolution and to others the possibility of it. Given the criticial situation of these nations, isn't violent revolution inevitable—whether your goals are equalitarian and socialist or bourgeois nationalist and reformist?

In these abstract terms the answer to the editor's question can go on for many pages and could, after all, be characterized as a matter entirely dependent on one's political point of view. We could have a civilized, reasonable exchange about our differences, the kind of chatty dialogue the mass media and the foundations sometimes sponsor. But the simple reply to the question of why all the talk about revolution in my report is that revolution is what the South Americans are talking about. Passionately. When such an idea gains currency among people, it is not going to be resolved by a round-table discussion, and that is why during the 1960s you had guerrilla movements springing up, being quashed, surfacing again. It would seem, as a Peruvian colonel told me, that even military repression will not hold them down.

There is, then, a whole area of reporting that is not concerned with the facts of elections and coups, the recital of events, names and dates, which is what seems to interest news editors most. This last leaves people unsatisfied, and they ask, "But what is it really like?" The only way to get close to that is to tell them, like our friend returned with his camera from the tour of the capitals of Europe, what you saw and what you heard. Simple descriptions; the development of the social sciences has made us forget they are basic. If the conclusions of a social study do not square with this palpable reality, something has gone wrong, and it is necessary to touch home base again. That is why the writer must be devoted not to objectivity but to truth-telling; he must supply the correctives to the theorists who have gone wrong. Not that I discount social scientists, if only because theorizing seems an activity necessary to the human mind, but I like to think they need our gossipy help.

For example, it is imperative that the reporter in South America tell us that revolutionary activity and revolutionary talk is as prevalent as it is. Since the death of Che Guevara, political scientists and Latin Americanists have concluded that revolutionary guerrillas have failed in Latin America, and this failure has received extraordinary coverage. (Flashes of glee illuminate some of the arguments, a kind of off-stage lighting that the audience can only subliminally perceive.) So much so that hardened as I am, by my experience in Cuba, against the generalizations current among us about Latin America, I expected, when I started on my trip last fall, to find at least a lull in revolutionary activity everywhere, such as I did find in Peru. Also, a reluctance to talk about it.

One of the arguments used to prove why Che had to fail was his and his band's lack of consideration for the strong national sentiments of the Bolivians. Of course, distance should not keep us from the knowledge that there is historical precedent, in Bolivar and many others, for South

Americans being actively concerned in the liberations of one another's countries—Che in Cuba is not a negligible case either—but one needs to see at first hand that this tradition is not handed down by some sort of racial unconscious but learned anew by each generation of school children. I knew too that, unfamiliar as we are with their history, we tend to think any revolutionary activity can only be imported; just as in the case of Cuba many Americans decided the revolution was anomalous or a sleight of hand by Fidel Castro because they were unaware of the century of struggle that preceded it.

Sometimes observation at first hand confirms what documents tell us. Many of the arguments used against Che were matters that he had already considered, and I had the feeling often, when reading the post-mortems of his adventure, that his critics had not done their homework— not read, for example, his "Message to the Tri-Continental." In it he writes at length about the difficulties of the guerrilla struggle, the many obstacles guerrillas must overcome, the years of fighting it must involve. He particularly emphasized the reverses that must be undergone—reverses necessary to find the right tactics for each situation—and I have no doubt that he would have characterized the defeat of his group as simply one such instructive example. A tough-minded man, he was called a romantic by his gleeful gravediggers, but it is they who are illusionists—which is what they mean by romantic—though crabbed ones, to be sure.

About nationalism Che had been clear. In the "Message," written while in Bolivia, he says, "In this continent practically only one language is spoken (with the exception of Brazil, with whose people those who speak Spanish can easily make themselves understood, owing to the great similarity of both languages). There is also such a great similarity between the classes in these countries that they have attained identification among themselves of an *internacional americano* type, much more complete than in the other continents. Language, customs, religion, a common foreign boss unite us. The degree and the form of exploitation are similar for both the exploiters and the men they exploit in the majority of the countries of Our America. And rebellion is ripening swiftly in it."

How interesting, then, to find Brazilians interrupting what had been a purely literary discussion to confess that they had yet to catch up with nineteenth-century Latin American writers. "It is only in the last decade that we have begun to read them. And we are working our way back. Until then we were closer to the culture of the United States and Europe—we did not feel South American." From that point the conversation became totally political. The young revolutionaries raise the subject directly; they have, apparently, close ties with their counterparts in the continent, particularly with the Tupamaros. The ideologues of the Brazilian military dictatorship subscribe, of course, to the nationalist rationale for the failure of Che, but the regime nevertheless polices very carefully their frontier with Uruguay; the youth traveling between the two countries get the closest scrutiny.

Time was when exiles from a regime such as has been in power in Brazil since 1964 would all have gone to Europe. Now you will find them in other Latin American capitals too. In Santiago de Chile you can spend an evening with Brazilians, Argentinians, Uruguayans, Venezuelans, and Chileans, and find less differences among them than between Texans and northerners. Brazilians at first took me for an Argentinian, Chileans for a Uruguayan, Peruvians

for a Chilean, but to all I was "one of ours." I sneaked a
look at a letter of introduction that a Brazilian gave me to
a Peruvian, and that was the phrase he used to describe
me.

In parentheses, this was not only an acknowledgment of
or a tribute to my Ybor City background; they also meant
that I was not a Yankee of State Department persuasion.
Oddly enough, I have found anti-Yankeeism to be less prevalent among left-wingers and revolutionaries. Because
they are class conscious, they make a distinction between
the American people and their government. I admit that
they may sound perfunctory and formal in statements of
this kind made for publication, but their beliefs do seem to
carry over into personal behavior. With them, individual
Americans are not the objects of their opposition to our
war in Viet Nam, say, or to our country's racism, whereas
nonrevolutionaries, particularly in England and France,
are indiscriminate in their anti-Yankeeism, an attitude that
American liberals often mistakenly attribute to a high-
minded disapproval of the worst elements in our culture,
when in fact it is due to a national chauvinism com-
pounded of snobbery and envy.

The nonexclusiveness among Latin Americans of revolutionary persuasion modifies—whether or not it altogether
disproves—what the theorists have told us about the post-
Che period on the continent. Until such time as revolutionary armies cross the frontiers, as Che obviously hoped
would occur when his guerrilla band took root and multi-
plied, you cannot prove that the same language, customs,
religion, and foreign boss do unite the continent. Not in
the ultimate sense. Yet I do not know how any reporter
who talked to South Americans last fall could have failed
to note the revolutionary potential of their oneness. Or

having met even so weak an underground group as the Movement of the Revolutionary Left in Chile, not learn that they are girding themselves for a long struggle. Or seeing that so many are willing today to risk their lives or being captured and tortured, not wonder how many to-morrow will move from verbal to armed opposition.

The second anniversary of Che's death took place while I was in South America, and so many were the acts to commemorate his death—from peaceful meetings to sabotage and plane hijacking—that it was plain that his example spoke to the whole continent. His stature as a great leader of the Latin Americans is indisputable; even the Right cannot attack him frontally. One columnist of a conservative newspaper in Chile used the extraordinary argument to denounce acts of sabotage by revolutionaries that this was no way to honor the memory of a great man, because Che would have disapproved of such actions. Everyone else joked that in 1970 anyone wanting to visit Cuba need only board any plane in Latin America on October 8—it was bound to be hijacked.

If one expects, from having read our commentators, that after the defeat of Che's band there would be a lull not only in activity but in sentiments of this kind, it is even more likely that there would be, after years of isolation, less sympathy for Cuba. The opposite is true. The blockade has been overcome—students, political leaders of the Left, intellectuals, and artists have managed to visit Cuba —and the Cuban revolution means to them that they too can make theirs. In abstract historical terms one should have known that the dynamics of that revolution would not be contained by the blockade we have imposed. I should not have been surprised, had our newspapers influenced me less.

In some ways the experience of my hometown, Ybor City, in relation to the Cuban revolution has been the same as Latin America's. Most of the colony, particularly those of Cuban descent, were in sympathy with it, open and full in 1959, surreptitious now and almost invisible to those who are not of the same beliefs. The Latin American countries were forced to break commercial and diplomatic relations with Cuba, and the counterpart of this campaign in Ybor City, waged by the F.B.I. and the Cuban exiles, against the oldtimers involved intimidation, red paint-splattered homes, and loss of jobs. But whenever Fidel Castro speaks there are innumerable radios in Tampa tuned to Radio Havana, at a low volume.

A cousin of mine likes to act out a wonderfully funny scene, a kind of rerun of herself listening with mock sympathy to a Cuban exile neighbor, who has trapped her while watering the lawn, complaining that Tampa Latins have little empathy for the exiles' troubles. The climax comes with the exile's confession that he fears there are many Communists among Tampa Latins and my cousin's horrified exclamation, "How terrible!" My mother's response to the defeat of the Bay of Pigs invasion was to recall to me my grandfather who, although he lived his whole life in Tampa, had been a Cuban patriot. "If only he were alive today," she said. "He would have been so proud!" These are, I think, important happenings, and someone should report them.

In Santiago de Chile Angel Parra singing his "Song to Cuba" was a significant event of that order. He plays it a lot these days, and I heard him the evening I visited the folk-song night club I mention in the chapter on Chile. The lyrics of the song are, in the main, a description of the despairing life of the people of Chile, and Parra uses old-fashioned images for this—the worker taking to drink, the mother wearing herself out washing clothes, the son becoming a thief. The lines, however, are taut and the alliterations and puns clever. "How long will this continue, compañero?" he asks. "And don't tell me you can vote. The only thing you're throwing away is your life." In Spanish the verb "to vote" also means "to throw away." He concludes:

> So when I see my son
> Sit and watch the sea,
> I tell him there's one country
> That reigns over its immensity—
> That queen's name is Cuba
> And this song is for her!

There are two moments during the song when the audience cannot contain itself—the jibe at elections and the tribute to Cuba.

What I have been trying to suggest here, and elsewhere in this book, is that the Cuban revolution is an irrepressible issue and a dynamic factor in South America. The attitude toward elections is an example. In our country, critics of Fidel Castro took up his failure to hold elections after the Batista regime was militarily defeated as a way of condemning him; the Cubans' audacious reply was that elections do not reflect the will of the people and are only a means by which to distract and deflect it. Their argument fell on sympathetic ears in Latin America, not only because ours sounded specious, since governments friendly to us have usually come to power by other means; but because the Cubans' statement revived among radicals a distrust of elections that had been prevalent in the days preceding the launching of popular front tactics by the world Communist movement. In our hemisphere, Cuba has challenged not only United States hegemony but also the Soviet Union's ideological prescriptions of peaceful coexistence and peaceful transition to socialism.

I must not, however, exaggerate the influence of Cuba on the political tactics or even goals of Latin American reformists and revolutionaries. Guerrilla tactics and anti-imperialist struggles preceded the Cuban revolution, and their independence movements have a long, honorable history, but the Cuban revolution and the writings and example of Che Guevara (inseparable phenomena) are now entwined with the history and revolutionary present down there. The fight between the Cuban Communist Party and the orthodox parties of Latin America, who take their line from the Soviet Union, has endless reverberations. In Chile, for example, the French film *La Guerre Est Finie* became the vehicle for a heated political debate still echoing last fall.

For us, *La Guerre Est Finie* was memorable for several reasons, not the least of which was Alain Resnais' startling yet natural technique of projecting visually the thoughts of his characters, not through fade-outs accompanied by mood music showing us that we were proceeding toward the visualization of an inner state, but by clean cuts, as if we were being taken from one action to another. This technique had the wonderful effect of depicting in images what we know emotively: that our thoughts and hopes are an inextricable, real part of any given scene, of equal weight, in fact, with our actions. Perhaps of greater interest was the hero's story as emissary of the Spanish Communist Party in exile (though the specific party was not made clear) to work clandestinely in Spain. These scenes evoked great nostalgia for the unacceptable conclusion of the Spanish Civil War, and the hero's return to Spain, perhaps to die, meant for most that the good fight must go on, even when the tactics are mistaken, as the hero knows.

In Chile, the film was taken, by its admirers and critics, as an attack on the old Communist parties, the authoritarian tactics of their leadership, and their separation from the real conditions of their constituency. It was common knowledge that Jorge Semprun, the scenarist, had led a life like that of his hero; he is the son of Spanish exiles, educated in France, and operated for a long time clandestinely in Spain—he was, in fact, the famous "Carlos" who eluded the Franco police. He was also a member of the central committee of the Spanish Communist Party, and finally, in disagreement with the policies of its exile members, left it. All this entered into the debate about the film in Chile, and Chilean Party spokesmen went so far as to accuse Semprun of having revealed, through the film, organizational details that required the restructuring of the Spanish Party's clandestine organization to protect it from the Franco police. This was not true, of course, but it showed to what lengths the orthodox Communists were willing to go—just as they remained silent about Cuba for several years, when defense of it was a necessary task of Latin Americans—to protect their political line from the criticisms of their New Left.

In Chile the film was transformed, and I have taken time to tell about it in order to show that describing "what it is really like" forces one to see it as the South Americans do. The failure of Che's Bolivia group and the Cuban line on guerrilla warfare as the path to revolution—at our distance from that continent and with the kind of information we receive, both seem to have failed—has to be lived from down there. What has happened to that is also, in part, a transformation; part, the surprises that life always springs on any theory. In the latter category fall the developments in

Peru and Bolivia. In Che's lifetime, there might have been reason to doubt one thesis that was subsumed by the argument for guerrilla warfare—that the nationalist bourgeoisie had not the interest or capacity to make any Latin American country independent of the United States. This might have been debated but certainly not that the military could become the agency for reform. That was out of the question. Yet Peru and Bolivia would seem to disprove it, and it was as much a surprise to Latin Americans as to our State Department. It is interesting to consider, as is suggested in the chapter on Peru, that one element of inspiration for the militarists were those guerrillas who tried to implement Che's line in Peru.

More interesting is the development of urban guerrillas, a phenomenon unforeseen by Che. Yes, he believed that the cities should be organized, but mainly in support of the guerrillas in the countryside. To some this emphasis of his meant a lack of faith in the urban working class, but it is more likely that the mobility the countryside affords for the essentially hit-and-run tactics of the guerrillas was decisive. Also, the Cuban experience. The urban guerrillas of Montevideo, Sao Paulo, Rio de Janeiro, and now La Paz and Santiago have yet to move out of the first stage of nuisance and sabotage activities and rival the regime's police or army for control of some area of the country, but in the goals they have selected thus far they have been successful and persistent. While I was in South America, the Tupamaros made what seemed the first attempt to enter into a larger sphere of action—they held a small town near Montevideo for almost an hour in a clever maneuver initiated from the capital. All of these groups believe they must spread out of the cities—without abandoning them or relegating them to a supportive role—to establish full-scale guerrilla movements in the countryside, but even if they are successful in this, it would still be a reversal of the plan of action Che promoted.

Che also exempted countries like Uruguay and Chile as scenes for armed struggle, because their democratic institutions still afforded their citizens peaceful means for change and reform—or, in any case, fostered the illusion that peaceful progress was possible. When you get the leader of the underground in Chile saying that one hundred years of democracy have left the country in no better state than the nations that have lived through a series of dictatorships, a new ideological element has begun to make its way. He is saying that capitalism with or without democracy feels the same to the oppressed. Only two years since the death of Che and there have been so many changes. Yet he continues to be the great "impulsor," the inspiration of the revolutionary cadres, and his example erases national boundaries. Can all this be called a lull in interest in revolutions? Can it even be called a defeat for Che?

Selective and determined reading of our newspapers might have gotten the American reader many of these facts, but little sense of what weight to give them. He would have done better with the "Rockefeller Report on the Americas," which does have to face facts, because it is supposed to help the Republican administration in formulating future policy, to use a phrase with which its writers would feel comfortable. To serve its purpose it had to both jolt and soothe, a function that is reflected in its style, always reaching out for Jeffersonian rhetoric and falling back on corporatese. In a high-minded preamble, it tells you that the mission "went to visit neighbors and found brothers"; elsewhere that it conducted "saturation visits." This unevenness of tone is characteristic of the sadly divided report, a kind of cross-eyed view of Latin America.

Governor Rockefeller and his enormous staff of almost one hundred visited twenty countries—Chile, Peru, and Venezuela asked him please not to come—during the spring and summer of 1969, and to each nation some twenty-five of this revolving staff went along. There were seventeen listed in the report as the "advance group," and it would, therefore, not seem an idle boast that the mission met, as Governor Rockefeller's prefatory letter to President Nixon states, not only with heads of state and officials but also leaders "both public and private." Strange that Senhora Niomar Bittencourt, about whom I write in the chapter on Brazil, should have been overlooked; a wealthy woman who founded Rio de Janeiro's museum of modern art and who is also owner-editor of one of the city's leading newspapers, she was also an old friend of the governor's. True, she was a vocal opponent of the military dictatorship and had been jailed earlier in the year, but she certainly should have qualified for the curiously worded category of private leader. Perhaps the reason can be found in the foreword (the report bristles with prefatory letters, preambles, forewords, subdivisions of all kinds, like corporate memos to the board of directors) where Governor Rockefeller talks of "this fruitful opportunity to listen to the responsible people" of those countries. "Responsible people" is a flexible phrase: it can be stretched—or rather, contracted—to exclude taxi drivers and Senhora Bittencourt, both of whom I'd rather listen to than any head of state in those twenty countries.

But enough coy disingenuousness on my part. The report tells us that we are not liked in Latin America and that relations with its countries have deteriorated so much

that if we do nothing we may be isolated from the continent in the next decade. We have "tried to direct the internal affairs of other nations to an unseemly degree,
thinking, perhaps arrogantly, that [we] knew what was
best for them." It says, "United States management, capital and highly advertised products have played a dispro-
portionately visible role," and later adds that "special
interests" may have exercised an unfavorable influence in
the distribution of American aid. The bureaucratic tangle
in Washington, it reports, is such that no matter how well
conceived policy decisions may be, they are exceedingly
difficult to carry out. These and many other sins of ours
should come as no surprise to the reader of the report, for
a kind of Jeffersonian preamble had mourned that "we
have lost sight of the values which are the real source of
our greatness."

The picture given of the internal situation of Latin
American nations is worse, for the reader must draw the
inescapable conclusion that in our relationship with them
we may suffer in the spirit but they indubitably suffer in
the flesh. Unstable governments, a population growth that
outstrips available jobs, illiteracy, malnutrition, injustices
of all sorts, plague the Latin Americans; and as accom-
paniment to them, "the ever-present disruptive forces
ready to exploit those who are uncertain and to stir up
those who are restless." This last is a theme that is struck
often, always on the bass drums, ominously. Elsewhere:
"Forces of anarchy, terror and subversion are loose in the
Americas." "The inflation, urban terrorism, racial strife,
overcrowding, poverty, violence, and rural insurgency are
all among the weapons available to the enemies of the
systems of the free nations of the Western Hemisphere."

So great seem the total of problems the South Americans face, the disrepute to which we have fallen, and the

errors we have made that it would seem logical if the report suggested that we let American companies fend for
themselves, turn our backs on the whole continent, and
show as little interest in it as if it were a Scandinavian
country. But no, the report reassures us several times, all
these problems are amenable to solution. The proposals
for helping the responsible South Americans help themselves turn out to be the usual ones, except for two considered by the newspapers as controversial and a problem
to the Republican administration. These were a reorgani-
zation of "the foreign policy and operating structure of
United States government dealing with the Western Hemisphere" that would presumably untangle the bureaucratic
mess; and the setting up of tariff preferences for import of
industrial products from Latin America, spurring their
consumer industries to prosper and create jobs. Neither
seems a convincing solution for the continent's disastrous
situation, unless given considerably more time than the
Latin American people are willing to wait.

So unconvincing, in fact, that on reflection one begins to
suspect that the writers of the report were not persuaded
either. Perhaps for this reason, they have headed their
"Policy and Action" section with the recommendation that
we not worry ourselves with the kind of militaristic and
repressive governments that we support in Latin America;
and followed this with a proposal for "Western Hemisphere Security" that would make it easier for us to create
two, three, many Viet Nams. This part of the report received little or no publicity but is, I think, the heart of it.
Six months after the report was handed to President
Nixon the administration had yet to take up any of its
recommendations, and it may be that out of skittishness
about the two "liberal" proposals, it may have missed the

opportunity to prepare more efficiently for the coming revolutions.

The proposal on western hemisphere security would establish a Western Hemisphere Security Council, directed by civilians, "to cope with the forces of subversion that operate throughout the western hemisphere." Someone with public relations experience must have added the following cautionary note: "Although the United States would have membership in the Council, the Council should have its headquarters outside of our country." Second, it is recommended that a "Western Hemisphere Security Training Assistance Program" be set up, and again the PR man must have added, "The name 'Military Assistance Program' should be dropped because it no longer reflects the security emphasis we believe important." Third, under the heading "Internal Security Support," it is proposed that we "respond to requests for assistance of the police and security forces of the hemisphere nations by providing them with the essential tools to do their job." And our old friend adds that we "should no longer maintain the permanent military missions in residence in other nations which too often have constituted too large and too visible a United States presence." Finally, the report approves our lifting the restrictions of sale of military equipment that we do not think they need, which the Conte and Symington amendment tried to do by reducing our aid program to those that insisted, to placate the militarists. We seem to know who our allies are going to be in the repression of revolutions.

Having come this far in trying to make plain what I saw in Latin America, I must confess to a certain despair. I am caught between the desire to change my countrymen's attitude toward these nations and the knowledge, as

Sartre said, that books do not make anything happen. Not in the immediate sense, anyway, and the help the Latin Americans need from us to avoid there being two, three Viet Nams is urgent. I am convinced that the only thing that can prevent them is the reversal by the American people of our government's use of its diplomatic and military power to sustain and further the economic interests of American corporations on the continent. Only this can free the energies of Latin Americans—from reformers to revolutionaries—to work to change in a positive way the misery of their present situation. Without this, all the talk of helping them to help themselves is at best paternalistic cant; at worst, another means of maintaining our presence there. Mine is a large order yelled into the wind.

I am reminded of two off-the-record discussions I attended in late 1968 and early 1969 in New York on the subject of our relations with Cuba. They were held by a foundation said to be financed by Rockefeller money and by most of the corporations and banks with investments in South America, and it was considered a rather bold departure for the foundation to be sponsoring exchanges that might encourage revision of our policy toward Cuba. One interpretation of their action was that they were being used by "State Department liberals" to test public opinion in this way, but whatever their motives the holding of the conferences was laudable.

To each gathering some fifteen people were invited. A varied group: journalists, academicians, businessmen, diplomats; experience and knowledge of Cuba the common denominator. Two or three on each occasion were persons, like me, who could be characterized as sympathetic to the Cuban revolution; some who had served in Washington were apologists for past policies. All of us were addressing ourselves to a paper prepared by a Latin Americanist which proposed, after an examination of some of the obvious failures of the blockade, a series of measures, ultimately leading to the re-establishment of diplomatic relations, to change our policy toward Cuba. The motives of the paper were neither moral nor materialistic; no change of heart toward the Cuban regime nor any economic benefits accruing to us were involved. It was simply a *Realpolitik* approach, meant to disengage us from practices that made us the object of criticism—even ridicule—in most of the world.

It was interesting to see that those without professional ties to business and banks were agreed, in varying degrees, to a change of policy. The businessmen and bankers were adamant. (One more piece of evidence for my belief that vulgar, Manichean Marxism is still a useful analytic tool in our country.) The superb exception to this rule was an elderly diplomat, now retired and consequently devoted to a defense of his life's work, who reacted apoplectically to the heresies he was hearing in that civilized conference room. "If it was not for this thing in Viet Nam," he said, the cane between his knees shaking with anger in a way that his body could no longer manage, "we would have gone into that island and thrown those Communists into the sea!"

Books do not make anything happen, but we do not cease from mental strife. My stepson, who is an activist in what his generation calls the Movement, will not have me believe in Sartre's statement. "If you believe that," he says, "you're just another petit-bourgeois writer." Nor will he accept as part of my argument his own thesis that it was not the teach-ins nor the educational activities of the peace movement that have made opposition to the war grow to such proportions in our country—it was the extraordinary Tet offensive of the Vietnamese two years ago that taught us we could lose the war. No, he says, what you write is part of the struggle.

So I shall pull myself out of my pessimism and try one last argument. The Rockefeller report says on page 131 (did anyone read that far?) to explain its proposal for a public health program in South America:

> The campesino goes to bed hungry every night of his life. He will probably never see a doctor, a hospital, a dentist, or a nurse. He has little hope of being vaccinated against smallpox, or inoculated against typhoid, tetanus, or yellow fever. If he becomes ill, there is no medicine; he trusts to fate that he will either get better, or die.

The opposite is true in revolutionary Cuba, and I must add that the *campesino* long ago was the object of a campaign that wiped out illiteracy and that the last time I was there the Committees for the Defense of the Revolution were trying to convince him that he should study nights and get up to a sixth-grade level. His children's opportunities are as great as anyone's in the country, and I shall not forget the nine- or ten-year-old black boy, at the arts school outside Havana, take the first position stance of ballet in front of me and say with a country accent, "I shall be the greatest dancer in Cuba!" When I saw the huge areas where the poor have squatted in Brazil, Chile, and Peru— the *favelas* in Rio, the *poblaciones* in Santiago, the slums in Lima that the authorities call *pueblos jovenes* (young towns)—I knew that any of the people living there would joyfully exchange places with the poorest of the poor in Cuba.

Above all, the Cubans live as if they were in command

of their destinies. For this reason, I have placed first in
this book my report on the young people in Cuba. Despite
the country's shortcomings, and some of the criticisms that
can be made of it, there exists an ambience of hope and
accomplishment that may suggest to the reader that there
is perhaps a solution to the problems of the Latin American nations described in the chapters that follow.

II
Cuba Under
Twenty-Five

In 1960, during my first visit to Cuba after the revolution, people in Havana explained, not entirely in jest, that the young fighters of the Sierra Maestre, now fully in command of the government, were pleased that they had found in President Osvaldo Dorticos, a forty-year-old lawyer, a man to head the government who was mature in years. Fidel was thirty-one when he came to power in 1959, Che twenty-nine, Raul twenty-six. By this gauge it will be some time before Fidel can be called an elder statesman, but in 1968 he advised Cubans that they should get rid of him when he grows old. No one took that seriously—except as confirmation, if any were needed, that the revolution is committed to the young, that the tone of its ideology and the success of its economic development of the island relies on the enthusiastic participation of the young.

Whether the generation that has grown up since the revolution wants this role on the terms that the still youthful leaders of the revolution extend to them is another matter. I spent three weeks talking to young people, and to older people about young people, in Havana, the Isle of Pines, the provinces of Las Villas and Camaguey; and what follows is a description of these encounters. Simply that; not a sociological study with carefully evaluated conclusions, nor the account of a suspenseful adventure; only talks with young people in those places where they are to be found. One warning: in the attempt to be representative, I may have given more space to the dissatisfied than their numbers warrant, and selected only conversations and activities that reflect Cuba's political trends.

Having decided that in the Cuban context youth begins at thirteen and ends at twenty-five, I sometimes felt I was suffering from double vision: talking to the teachers of a school for adolescent boys on the Isle of Pines, most of whose students were delinquent and came there as discipline problems, I realized with something of a start that the teachers themselves were twenty and twenty-one. Or discussing a trip to the interior with the Chief of Information of the Ministry of Foreign Relations, Teleforo Diaz, I learned that he is twenty-six. In this age span, then, can be found different levels of education, work, and commitment to the revolution.

One month before I arrived our newspapers carried the news, monitored from the Cuban radio, that there had been a roundup of large numbers of young people whom the Cubans characterized as Hippies: unshaven, unwashed, uninterested in work, outlandishly dressed by Cuban standards, they were given to hanging around La Rampa, a street that for a long time now has been the nighttime hub of the Vedado section of Havana. The Hippie phenomenon was several months old, but the authorities took action only when one small group broke into a high school, destroyed television sets used as teaching adjuncts in classrooms, and tore down photographs of Che. Without warning, the police ringed those blocks and, without discrimination, led everyone in the streets into Leyland buses and drove them off to the police stations; once there, anyone with proof that he or she worked, or belonged to a mass organization, was immediately released; those kept were sent off to state farms, where work and study, the Cuban cure for all ills, is expected to rehabilitate them.

When I arrived, the subject was still fresh, and one anecdote (probably apocryphal) illustrates the Cuban economic situation, the administration of justice, and the Cubans' attitude toward both. Down the street from the Capri Hotel, where many of the so-called Hippies gathered, is a candy shop where people queue for as long as three hours to buy fifty cents' worth of candy; the night of the roundup two old ladies on line were gathered up, taken to the police station, released; undaunted by the experience, they returned to the queue and successfully claimed their old place on the line.

To understand the young in Cuba today—or, in fact, anyone—you need to know that it is going through its worst period of scarcities. Everything is rationed, and often the items you are entitled to do not show up in the stores. The cities, particularly Havana, suffer from this situation most. To get into a restaurant you have to queue up the previous day for several hours in order to be given a *turno* for the next evening's meals. These urban scarcities (outside Havana everyone eats better and the students and farm workers are well fed) are, in a sense, artificial: agricultural production is up, but all of it, plus the fishing fleet's haul, is sold to pay for factories and machinery to put the agricultural economy on a scientific and highly productive level; a kind of forced capital accumulation that they expect will begin to pay off in 1970. In the spring all bars and nightclubs were closed; today movies are all open, but there are very few plays being done. There is, in fact, very little to do for entertainment, and the queues at the Coppelia, a giant, outdoor ice-cream parlor at the head of the Rampa, have become a place for banter, flirting, and passing the time until the early hours of the morning.

Walking in old Havana, where word has it the Hippies not rounded up have now scattered, I ran into a young painter I knew from previous visits. "They have all cut their hair and modified their clothes," he said, and stopped to greet three youngsters, two boys and a girl. They looked startled, muttered something, and walked away, their version of the put-down. We were joined by a poet (twenty-one years old) who had just published his first book and an actor (twenty-two), and for a while, sitting at an outdoor cafe on Cathedral Square, where tea was the only item, they talked about the Hippies and themselves.

"Of course the Hippies are a negative phenomenon," said the poet, "but a negative response to a negative situation. For young people there is a totally repressive situation, there is no way in which they can express their interests, no outlets for them. The army hangs over them all, and they are ferociously afraid of it. There are no clothes, no music and dance they can indulge, no freedom from the old deadly moral tradition. Do you know that this country has had a revolution and yet its morality is Christian through and through? Isn't that absurd?"

The actor: "And the idiotic thing is they work so hard to maintain things that are only a waste of energy. First, there is no need to talk so much about socialism, to din it into people's ears, when Cubans are innately socialist, people who share everything spontaneously, gladly. Second, all that puritanical propaganda to a people that is so sensual and sexually tolerant. You tell a Cuban that so-and-so is a homosexual and he will say, Is that so? and shrug his shoulders.

The poet: "They do not understand that young people are not interested in the future. Only in the immediately enjoyable—all those things you and I can do without—and it is this the revolution takes away from them. And offers them only work, work, work! So these groups started up here and in all the cities—it was becoming a big thing, anarchist, anti-intellectual, totally innocent, naive, a world of their own. They held their own fiestas—in private homes, even with the permission of the police. You know that here you need permission for everything—"

The painter: "Come now, you only have to speak to the block committee and warn them you are going to make some noise."

The poet: "They called them *Las fiestas de la papa.* Each one came in costume and carried a potato in his hand. I must say I liked the Hippies, even if I could never be one of them. . . ."

The actor: "You understand that the four of us here would never be accepted. The fact that we read a book or wrote one—that is enough."

The poet: "So innocent they were, there was even one group that called itself *El Tercer Mundo*. What do they know about the Third World—the concept, the political significance of it? It simply sounded appropriate to them. I spent time with them because—oh, for a whole series of reasons."

The painter: "He means sexual freedom."

The poet: "For *desahogo*, to be at ease. I do not care about scarcities or queues. I do not care about any of the material things but the freedom to be oneself."

We were quiet a moment after that statement. It was late and Cathedral Square, lit mainly by the moon now that electricity is being conserved, was silvery and serene. We heard a window open and water splash on the cobbles of the square, and all of us laughed: that old African rite of flinging water out of the house to keep evil spirits away while the family sleeps was still being observed. Just as surprisingly, the poet blurted, "You know that I can never be anticommunist. I cannot help being a socialist or for this revolution!"

Two days later I was again discussing the Hippies (pronounced *heepies*) with two other Cubans. They were very different young men, and so was the scene. It was the Isle of Pines, an island as large as the province of Havana and directly south of it, the inspiration for Robert Louis Stevenson's *Treasure Island* and also a favorite of Hart Crane's. Since early 1967 it is always called the Isle of Youth in the newspapers, for there then began a project for its development and colonization that the government boasts will make it the first communist community in

Cuba. Until then the revolutionary government had not paid much attention to it, except to station on it much of its army and firepower, for it was there they expected the United States invasion, not at the Bay of Pigs.

Not conceded by us to Cuba until 1925, its population never exceeded seven thousand, and its citrus groves were developed by Americans, all of whom have left. The project for its development was proposed by the Young Communists, and they recruited some forty-two thousand young volunteers, mainly from the provinces of Havana and Oriente, to come and work for two years. The land undulates more than Florida's and the horizon is broken by hills, but like Florida it is ideal for citrus and cattle, two products much in demand not only in socialist but also in European capitalist markets where Cuba is anxious to earn hard currency to pay for machinery, trucks, and buses. Less than two years after the project began, the number of cattle and endless rows of young citrus trees one sees everywhere is impressive. You cannot see their fruits in the stores on the mainland; in the island's processing and packing plant the cardboard cases were all printed in English and French, and the machinery to handle next year's enormously increased yield was bought from Italy.

The young people who came here lived, at first, under semimilitary regulations, but although they still live mainly in barracks, there are no restrictions on their comings and goings. Those who did not adjust to the hard work and discipline have long ago left, and those who remain are highly enthusiastic young people who give the island the energetic ambience of a frontier society. "Of course, they are happy," said the chauffeur who drove me around the island, "they do not have parents here to advise them constantly—and they have sexual freedom!" All their needs—food, lodging, clothes, transportation—are supplied free, and their salaries (sixty to eighty pesos a month, depending on whether they have dependents) go for movies and dinners and ice cream in Nueva Gerona, the capital and port which has been transformed, according to old inhabitants.

Early in 1967, the young people spent their late afternoons and evenings in Nueva Gerona, after ten- to twelve-hour days on the farms, building parks, a theater, the Coppelia ice-cream parlor, restaurants, all as voluntary labor. Now from eight to eleven at night almost everyone is in a classroom studying, and the two young men with whom I discussed, among other things, the Havana Hippies were teachers in these makeshift, dimly lit classrooms. We were driving from Nueva Gerona southwest across the island to El Colony for dinner, a motel where we were staying, and the two, hoping to hitch a ride, stood near a sign that indicated that a left turn would take you to Free Algeria, one of the new collective farm towns. They too were headed for El Colony to pick up the laundry for their group of teachers who bunked in Free Algeria, laundry the motel staff had volunteered to do free on a regular basis. From the motel they planned to return with the bus that at seven-thirty made a round of that corner of the island for students whose classrooms were in Free Algeria.

I told them the waitresses at El Colony had invited me at breakfast to join them in their classes at night, and they were delighted. They sat with me around the motel's swimming pool; beyond was a private cove of a beach. All this had been meant for very different clients, since the motel, finished in 1958 and owned principally by Batista, was designed as a secluded gambling casino and an adjunct to an abortion clinic. The teachers, Pablo Jesus Suarez (twenty-three years) and Luis Cartaya (nineteen), were both in their last year of the Escuela Obrero-Campesino, and next year would matriculate at Havana University to begin careers in medicine and chemistry. Meanwhile they had come as volunteers with some eighty other E. O. C. students and their own professors to study during the day and to teach at night.

The E. O. C. schools are part of the many-pronged attack of the government to educate the population. They are still principally concerned with educating workers in evening schools, but in the last two years their best students have been offered the opportunity to study full time and retain, as scholarships, the salary of the jobs they give up. Pablo Jesus and Luis were such students; both were from Havana, Pablo Jesus from a middle-class family, Luis from a working-class one.

It was their belief that there was a counterrevolutionary core among the Hippies and that they corrupted and attracted more innocent ones who were simply interested in clothes and American music. They also offered recruits girls to sleep with, and introduced them to marijuana. Didn't it bother them, I asked, that these kids were summarily rounded up, not tried but sent off to farms, with none of the opportunities courts give them to defend themselves? No, they *knew* the authorities were just and can sift the criminal from the corrupt, the foolish from the innocent. "Listen, a girl friend of mine was picked up on the Rampa," said Luis. "She likes to wear very short skirts, but she works and shares none of the Hippie ideology, and as soon as she identified herself they apologized and released her."

"And work is the way to develop," said Pablo Jesus. "Work is everything."

While we talked, Luis kept scanning an outline on his lap for the mathematics class he was teaching that night, but he looked up when I asked if the activities all over Cuba that took young people away from the homes and parental guidance at crucial periods during their growing up might not be harmful. He shook his head vigorously. "Well, won't it at least make them love their parents less?" I asked.

"On no," he said. "No, I love them more and more. I have learned how much they went through—without the help the revolution gives us all now—to raise me."

"Are you *militantes*?" I asked, meaning if they were members of the Young Communists.

They shook their heads and looked at each other, and then Pablo Jesus confessed, "They are considering us now, our work is being reviewed. There is nothing we aspire to more than that."

When the school bus arrived, it had already picked up some young men from a military unit nearby, and they got out to help the teachers bring in their laundry; the chambermaids and waitresses joined us last for the ten-minute ride to Free Algeria. Another bus took a different route to bring young men from a cattle farm and girls from citrus groves to the new little stucco town—homes for families who had decided to settle there, a general store, a cafeteria, a barbershop, a primary school, a nursery for children of working mothers, an open-air theater. Classes were held in the primary school and in the wooden barracks building where a group of teachers bunked and studied during the day.

I went to one of the latter· for a class in Spanish in which an assortment of all these young people were taking a review course to allow them to start at a high school level next term. The walls were a worn green, the dim bulbs hung from a high ceiling, the blackboard was hard to make out, and for this class there were no books, so that the teacher had to read aloud or write on the board the rules of accentuation they were studying that night. The students copied the rules in pulpy notebooks with carefully guarded pencils—everything is scarce in Cuba—and never had to be called to attention. The teaching technique was old-fashioned (rules and examples; learning by rote) but none of these young people who had worked hard all day (some were cowboys) ever suppressed a yawn during the hour and a half. The classroom had the air of a moralistic nineteenth-century print: Abe Lincoln reading law by the light of a log fire.

The teacher, a classic Latin beauty, was no older than her pupils, and although her training sometimes gave her the tone of an oldtime schoolmarm, her manner was the open, equalitarian one of the Cuban revolution. "From the work you turned in last night," she began, "it seems to me that some of you, compañeros, have not grasped the concept of the synonym." And whenever she saw a doubtful face that night, she peered and asked, "Do you understand that, compañero? Are you sure?" At the end of the class, I searched her out and told her how wonderful it had been. "Really? Are you sure?" she asked, terribly pleased. "We have such a responsibility to make it worthwhile . . . most of them are going to be up working at six in the morning."

In the mathematics class, taught by Pablo Jesus, there were also older men who had settled with families in Free Algeria, and that evening they were reviewing the previous month's work for a major test the next night. Pablo Jesus began by saying that he was going to go over some examples of addition, multiplication, and division of relative numbers. A middle-aged Negro called out, "*Maestro*, you do everything you can there for me, because I cannot say that I am very clear on the subject." At eleven, Pablo Jesus announced that those who wanted to continue reviewing could remain for at least another hour and catch the last bus from Nueva Gerona that would go by at twelve on the highway. Three or four stayed; the rest of us piled into the bus that brought us. . . .

A tall, fair girl from El Colony sat behind me; in Spanish class she had gotten up energetically from her seat several times to write on the blackboard words exemplifying accentuation rules, and they were always ones like "guerrilla, revolution, communism." I told her and it surprised her. In a moment she and one of the soldiers began singing *La Era Está Pariendo Un Corazón*, which can be translated as *Our Time Is Giving Birth to a Heart* (I have tried other ways and it always sounds wrong in English), the number one pop hit whose composer Silvio Rodriguez (twenty-one years) I was to meet later in Havana. The others harmonized. "Do you like it here?" someone asked me, and I nodded. The fair girl immediately led the entire bus in *Qué Linda Es Cuba!—Cuba Is So Beautiful!*—as if to thank me. The next afternoon, she and another girl and the soldier sat out at the open-air bar and together studied for the math test.

That morning our car opportunely broken down at the entrance to a camp called La Patria (Homeland) whose girls all worked in the citrus nursery down the road, and I met Ana Garcia, one of its *responsables*, a widow in her late twenties, old for the Isle of Pines. We walked over to the nursery and, proud of her grafting knife, she showed me how they graft grapefruit and lime shoots on sour orange stems. Around us stretched many acres of neat rows of plants stopping only at the high hills where an old house perched. "That is El Abra," she said, taking for granted I would know that it was the home where Jose Martí was kept under house arrest as a student because he was too young to be imprisoned. "There are no more prisons on this island, you know." She put a hand to her head and said, as if there were some connection, "The way I see it, I do not begin to do for this revolution what it does for me."

I asked her if it was true that the relationships between men and women were different on the island. "Well, there are supposed to be seven men to each girl and that helps. It is very nice for the girls, because they can say to any fellow who gets dictatorial, You do not like it that way? —then goodbye, there is another one of you in line waiting." She laughed. "Of course I do not know where the seven who belong to me have gone!" Would she marry again? She became thoughtful. "I do not know if I will fall in love again and then it has to be some one who will let me lead my own life."

Ana came from Havana, and so did Luisa Herrera, a former stenographer and office worker I met at the Battle of Saigon, one of the many dairy farms on the island. She was twenty-three, divorced, has a year-old child with her parents in the city, and plans never to leave the island— "unless, of course, I am needed elsewhere," she added, like a good Young Communist. We sat on the fence around the milking shed, waiting for the cows to be brought in by cowboys who had also been city workers. She wore a polo shirt, pants, and high rubber boots. Also silver bangle bracelets. The shed was hosed down, the feed was in the troughs, she had time to talk. "All I had seen of a cow were the milk bottles in the stores."

I forced her to talk about the roundup of the Hippies. The subject made her laugh. "I tell you, we were all here when the news came and we said, at last, at last! I know that to wear those kind of clothes, to let one's hair grow, to refuse to wear a tie—all that in capitalist countries is a way of protesting bourgeois ways, those very correct clothes bourgeois men wear. But what is there to protest here? The war in Viet Nam? They have plenty of opportunities for that. Work, work, that is the only way to develop one's character and society and the revolution. Besides, our men dress like men, with their belts firmly around their waists, their clothes clean—that is the way we like them."

But what Luisa wanted to talk about were the cows, the characteristics of Holsteins and Cebus and the improved meat and milk yields that come with crossing the two; why the calves of the Cebus have to be tied to them during milking; how quickly a calf in a crowd finds its mother. "Though I still cannot tell which calf belongs to which cow!" and she laughed, enjoying the talk. The administrator—a young, undiluted black—came over and his face lighted up at her laughter and talk. Once he put a hand on her knee, another time an arm around her shoulders; she turned and smiled, completely unself-conscious: they were comrades, unusual for a white, office girl from Havana.

Luisa was happy that I would be visiting Los Internados de Pino Alto (the live-in students of Pino Alto school) because many of the 347 boys there (fourteen- and fifteen-year-olds) had once been unruly street kids from Havana, shoeshine boys, news vendors, boys without families; and she was sure the Hippies would turn out as good as they. The arch across the road entrance and the tiny guard room at the school were the only sign that it might be a disciplinary institution, but they looked merely decorative. The sign on the arch said "Forgers of the Future," and the two on guard duty were students, one of whom interrupted his reading of a Selma Lagerlof novel to remove the rope across the road. There were playing fields and flower beds beyond, and the low barracks-like buildings were painted white.

The school was run by the Ministry of Education and the Army, its director Lt. Roberto Alvarez Garcia, a thirty-three-year-old veteran of the Sierra Maestra, and its assistant director Isabel Otero, a twenty-one-year-old Makarenko (the name of the early Soviet educator is given to the young people who have taken a five-year crash course to become schoolteachers). I asked them immediately about the Vikings, the gang of boys the school had taken in, and Isabel raised her eyebrows to indicate they were hellfire. "At first they used to run away, and we would go look for them in the forest—" she began, but the lieutenant interrupted: "Listen, all those boys needed was affection. That name—Vikings—makes you think they were worse than they were, and when it comes right down to it they only committed the mischiefs of youth."

Isabel laughed. The lieutenant repeated, "They are good boys."

"Yes, they are," said Isabel. "They come to us with their most private problems, they call us mama and papa."

I looked at the lieutenant, and he nodded; I could well imagine what a potent father figure a revolutionary guerrilla like him must be.

I was unprepared for the classrooms where I sat with a sixth-grade class: models of deportment and participation. Not just because of me, for the neat piles of books and notebooks each student carried, all carefully covered with newspaper sheets, were in perfect condition, and the work they'd done in them was exemplary. The boys crowded round me after classes, before the afternoon's physical education activities, and there was nothing to suggest they'd ever been a problem to anyone.

They wanted to know if I had been at the Olympics in Mexico. One asked if it were true that the United States stole sports talent from other nations in order to come out ahead. I said I didn't think so, and to change the subject I said, "You know that quite a few Cubans have played in our big league baseball teams?" The boy called out, "That is what I mean—the imperialists stole them!"

"Is it really good here?" I asked. Oh yes!

"Does anyone run away to the forest?" Oh no!

"Is everyone going home for the Christmas holidays?" Yes, yes, yes!

Then one boy spoke with such intensity that it created a moment of quiet. "It must be said that this school is our home too," he said. "To me it is just like home."

The next day I ran into Isabel Otero in Nueva Gerona; she was on the way to Havana on leave, and so was Mario Benitez, a twenty-one-year-old Negro who was the *responsable* for the sixth-grade class. "Not a teacher, I simply live with them and advise them," he said. "There were 120 of us who came to the island with 1,500 such boys in 1967 and now, one year later, there is only need for twenty-eight of us."

I said I had not had an opportunity to ask them at school if they had not felt the need for a formal course or lectures on sex for these adolescent boys. Isabel's smile told me I was asking an unorthodox question and also one that she liked. She nodded. Mario seemed not to have

heard, so I asked differently, "Since the boys must come
to you with all sorts of questions, don't you feel a scientific
explanation—out in the open—would help?" Isabel simply
looked ahead this time, and Mario leaned his head on
one hand, looked down, then sideways at me and smiled:
he definitely wasn't going to discuss this with a girl
present.

In Havana, a day later, a music teacher in Cubanacan,
a complex of art schools in what was once the luxurious
Country Club section, talked about this problem with me.
She is an important composer, many of whose compositions are electronic, and is, of course, thoroughly sophisticated—and forthright. "Of course, it should be a course.
There they are, their bodies boiling, thrown in together
for days on end. Talk about male homosexuality—God
knows how many Lesbian relationships are being formed.
I talked to the director about this but of course if such a
course were given the parents might start pulling the kids
out of school. What a situation! Some Swedes visited me
recently—in sandals, bearded, terribly radical and political—and I talked to them about this to change the subject,
for I could see from their questions about my compositions
that they were not interested in music, just sociology. So I
said that sex education was needed if only to prevent
homosexuality, and they said it is a petit-bourgeois prejudice of mine, why should I care what form of sex they
enjoy. Petit-bourgeois—imagine! That is what they called
me." She laughed heartily, then added, "Of course, they
are right!"

That night I found a young man eager to talk about sex
prejudices. I stood at a queue at one in the morning at
Coppelia, the ice-cream parlor that occupies a square
block, and found the flirting there was more varied than I

had been led to expect. The young man, looking younger than his twenty-five years, gazed at my shoes, then pants and windbreaker, and said, "I am one of those who likes clothes." His pants were quite slim. "*Son Cubanos pero yo los enfermé*," he said; which literally means, *They are Cuban but I have made them ill.* Young men who like tight pants, sideburns, who pay too much attention to their clothes, are considered to have *la enfermedad*, the illness. I had heard that some boys had become adept at stitching in their pants legs when they left school in the afternoon and letting them out wide in the morning.

He was inspector of junior high school classes in Pinar del Río and was in Havana on vacation. In 1959 he began as a total enthusiast of the revolution, took a crash course to become a schoolteacher, was twice a "vanguard worker" in his school district. "Before we graduated we worked for a month in the Sierra, and Fidel came to our graduation. How beautiful that was!" he sighed. "I was once a Methodist, but now I do not believe in anyone." I waited. "If you believe in sexual freedom—well."

"Don't you believe in the revolution?"

"I am neither for it nor against it. In fact, I believe that a successful counterrevolution would be a disaster for the country. Oh, but the loss of spontaneity—now everything is organized."

"Is it very difficult for homosexuals?"

He gave me a quick look. "One has to be a little fictitious when you are in my position. To do my job right you should believe wholeheartedly in the revolution." Then he came to the point. "Homosexuality is on the increase, maybe because there is always such.a campaign against it—it attracts young people like forbidden fruit. And now homosexuals are more brazen, especially those

who were in the U.M.A.P. [work-prison camps for 'anti-
social elements' abolished in 1967]. They say, There is
nothing they can do to me that is worse than that."

He had heard that the Ministry of the Interior has a
group of very handsome young men who sleep with men
and then turn them in; also that in the universities, especially in the colleges of medicine and liberal arts, they weed
out homosexuals.

"It is very difficult to get into the university. You have to
pass oral examinations where every effort is made to deter-
mine that you are the kind of revolutionary they want.
They ask strange, surprising questions, such as, Describe
an average day in your life twenty years from now."

Next day, waiting in the lobby of the Habana Libre
(the old Hilton) for a friend who came two hours late
(the revolution hasn't changed that), I struck up a conversation that also led to this subject with Manuel Mariño,
a nineteen-year-old Havana University student, a mathematics major, who was waiting for a cousin. The cousin
had come from Oriente because only a Havana hospital
had a surgeon who could perform the operation he
needed. Across from us, a young man neither of us knew
raised his hand to get our attention, and said, "Compañero, that is a question of concept—there are people
who have that prejudice, they believe only Havana hospitals can cure them. Yet it is a fact that we now have many
fine hospitals in the interior. . . ." His name was Alejandro
Celada, a fifth-year medical student; a classmate, Modesto
Hernandez, a black from a small town in Pinar del Rio,
joined him, and the four of us talked for two hours.

My conversation with Manuel began when he saw me
peer at the issue of *Pensamiento Crítico*, a quarterly devoted to articles on political science, philosophy, psychol-

ogy, sociology, that he was reading. "This issue ran out immediately," he said. "We swooped down from the university and they were all gone in a couple of hours. It is the article on structuralism by Jean Cuisenier that interests me." He let me look at it. There were articles by Martin Nicolaus, Henri Lefebvre, and an interview with Roland Barthes. Manuel, it turned out, was also interested in films, the theater, and literature.

The medical students were not as literary as he, but they shared his enthusiasm for films, and they were soon in a discussion of a new Cuban one called *Lucia*, the first feature by a twenty-four-year-old director called Humberto Solas. All over Cuba young people seemed to be discussing its three sequences—the longest takes place in 1868, the others in 1933 and the 1960s—and although I had yet to see it, its stories had been described to me in detail at four in the morning, during the ferry ride to the Isle of Pines, by a group of young men. Each sequence revolves around the heroine and her changing social role in relation to revolutionary struggle. Interest in this theme separates the young from the middle-aged, as do its explicit sex scenes and naturalistic speech. One young man in Santa Clara said to me, "When my aunt saw all those naked runaway slaves on horseback fighting the Spaniards —well, she was scandalized!"

Manuel considered it an important film, but he criticized its lack of stylistic unity, and found the last story about the campesino woman unrealistic. "Believe me, I am from Oriente, and our campesino women may have been obedient in the past, but they never kept quiet. Certainly not now. Besides, it puts the whole question of women's rights under the revolution rather simplistically —imagine, having a campesino jealous of the alphabet-

izer! Do any of you know any alphabetizer to have received any but the most courteous, loving treatment?"

The students kept up on films and theater because they
can attend free. The movie theater across from the hotel
reserved Thursdays as the day university students can enter without paying. Passes for ballet and stage plays are
frequent. "They are no longer handed out to just the 'best'
students," Manuel explained, "or it would have become a
matter of only the *militantes* going. The passes simply go
to those who are most interested." The students, like the
workers on the Isle of Pines, get everything free and receive eighteen pesos a month for pocket money.

I told them what I'd heard about the difficulty of ma-
triculating, the weeding out of homosexuals, and about my
knowledge that two years ago it was the custom for
classes to meet in open assembly and purge from their
ranks counterrevolutionaries and homosexuals. "That is
not done that way anymore," said Alejandro. "There is a
faculty-student committee to handle disciplinary problems." He stopped and lowered his voice. "See that fellow
in the white shirt who just went by? He is a homosexual.
He was accused during our second year and he admitted
it. He could have continued at the university in another
field but chose not to. In our class there are two or three
—yes, three—homosexuals who were found out, and they
continue to study, only they will not be dealing with pa-
tients. They will be in research or other fields."

He sensed I was maintaining a certain amount of re-
serve, and added, "I do not know whether they are cured
—after all, very little is known scientifically about homosexuality and it is a subject of study—but they are not
immoral or scandalous people. Still, they are not allowed
to be in a position of dealing intimately with other persons
. . . you understand?"

I told Modesto, the only black of the three, that sympathetic observers have said that anti-black prejudice survives in Cuba. He looked at me as if I were joking. "Not openly," I said, "but in subtle ways; in standards of beauty, in failure to make a special effort with blacks so that higher positions in leadership and the professions do not fall mainly to whites."

"Absurd," said Modesto. "I have never run into a situation in which there has been any discrimination. Of course there are individuals—usually older people formed before the revolution—who have prejudices and they are hard to change. But young people? Never. And blacks are in all positions, anywhere you turn. I do not know what your friends mean by standards of beauty, but the beauties in the carnivals are of every shade of color."

Alejandro: "The best proof is that this is a subject you had to introduce. Has anyone in Cuba brought it up with you—no, right? And in the matter of love, you will see couples of every combination."

I said that although I hadn't talked to them, I knew there were blacks in the arts who—

Manuel interrupted: "I know about that *folklórico* group. I shall tell you something interesting about them— they are all older people!" He joined Modesto and Alejandro in their laughter: the word *older* had set them off.

That week the Committees for Defense of the Revolution, the mass organization which works at the block level, had been calling meetings to discuss whether the bars and nightclubs should reopen, and I understood the vote was overwhelmingly in favor. If they opened, it would be the first time that a measure to which Fidel had lent his verbal and moral support was rescinded. The three students looked at me, afraid to sound like puritans.

Finally, only the medical students spoke; perhaps because they were older and had some nostalgia to drown. "There was something wrong about the whole ambience," said Modesto. "I like women as much as anyone, but there was something false about meeting a girl on the Rampa and going to a club and having drinks and thinking how to get her to a place where you could have coitus. It put a different value on human relations."

"Right," Alejandro said. "I would walk over to the Rampa where everyone promenades and start a conversation with a girl and ask her to a club to have a drink. You know how the clubs were?" I nodded: some were so dark the waiters moved around with a flashlight which they aimed only at their feet. "There we would enjoy love or all the play of it short of coitus, and all the while there was this thing on my mind: is this love, is this girl *the* girl or is she like me. . . . No, it has to be different."

Outside Havana, the next day, I met a youngster whose approach to girls was more traditional. I had been accustomed on previous visits to Cuba to traveling on buses by myself, but this time I allowed the Ministry of Foreign Relations' press department to drive me out of Havana on two occasions, to save time. The car was a 1959 Cadillac which suffered blowouts and other breakdowns, the results of old age, worn tires, and unavailable spare parts. It aroused attention outside Havana, usually from young boys, and the three who inspected it in a filling station in Matanzas were typical.

After several turns around the Cadillac, their leader, a Negro thirteen years old, approached me. "Is this the only car of its kind in Cuba?"

I said no, and since he was now looking inside, I showed him how the windows opened and closed by pushbutton.

"With a car like this," he exclaimed, "the girls would be falling on top of me."

I asked him how many he would put in the car, and he started to count and then gave up. "As many as wanted to," he decided. "I would take them to *El Rincón Caribe* or Varadero Beach—oh my!" He leaned on the window and looked some more. "I think I had better settle for a Russian bicycle. I am saving my money for one."

On this trip I was headed for Siguaney, a tiny country town half way across the island in the hills of Las Villas; it is getting totally rebuilt because just outside it an enormous cement factory is nearing completion under Czech supervision; the hills around the factory will keep it supplied with raw material for a century. The young people who came to work there turned out be very much like those on the Isle of Pines, except that they talked cement and its use in dams and roads whereas the others had talked citrus and cattle. Many of them had come as part of the *Columna Juveníl de la Construcción* (the Youth Construction Column), an arrangement whereby trade school students are transferred with their teachers to projects such as Siguaney's to work and study at the same time.

By chance I ran into some whose presence there was an experiment: teenagers interested in music, theater, and art who for the first time were made part of the construction column. All but two (of the original fifty-three) plus one teacher had left the previous day after six months on the site. Besides working part-time on the factory, they studied and put on shows, concerts, and exhibitions for the workers. The two I met were part of the *artes plásticos* group who had stayed behind to pack the objets d'art they'd made for an exhibition to be shown in Havana.

Their Chilean teacher was very pleased with their six months of work; he showed me paint brushes made entirely by the boys from goat hairs, tin from evaporated milk cans, and twigs from a native bush; also enamel on copper ornaments and ashtrays that had been baked in a portable kiln. I trooped out with the three to a small ramshackle shed they'd built to cover a large kiln improvised with a gasoline drum buried in sand; it stood on a slope, and on the slanting side the bottom of the drum was exposed; under it there was a hole to build the fire. They brushed away the sand on top of the slope and lifted the top of the drum; inside were terra-cotta animals that had been baked the previous day.

"But how do you control the temperature?" I asked.

The boys pointed to their eyes. "By Eye-meter!" said the teacher. After we all laughed, the teacher said, "That has been the most valuable experience of all—making do with what we can find around, for there are shortages of art materials and kilns and these boys are now going back to their towns and teach others in the *Regionales de Cultura.*"

The *Regionales* organize amateur cultural activities in the towns, and the two boys had been active in Guanes, at the tip of Pinar del Rio, and so had a chance to volunteer for the project in Siguaney. One was twenty, the other twenty-one; both were the sons of campesinos. "And you will be content to return to Guanes?" I asked. They shifted their stances, put their hands in their pockets, and confessed, "It is our ambition to be accepted someday in Cubanacan, the art school in Havana."

I asked them if the local people and Siguaney workers had been attracted by the work of their group, and they pointed to a boy who'd been with us all along. He was not

quite sixteen and his father drove the bus that brought
workers from Cabaiguan, a nearby city, to the construction site. He'd come along one day for the ride and saw
the work of the cultural group and had immediately stuck
to them; the teacher had simply taken him in and let him
be part of the group. "I had always liked to draw," he said
to me. "But now I know it is my life."

Boys like them, for whom the extraordinary events of
1959 are dimly remembered happenings, do not offhand
point out that they owe to the revolution the unusual
course their own lives have taken. It was the same with
the boys in the park at Santa Clara where two years
earlier I had been held captive for five hours by a large
group who wanted to know, among other things, about
the Beatles and the Rolling Stones. I broke up my return
to Havana, after Siguaney, by stopping overnight in Santa
Clara, and as soon as I walked into the park, the traditional nightly gathering place for the youth, I was ac-
costed by one who remembered me. Now the Beatles
were being played on a loudspeaker that could be heard
all over the park, there were more unescorted girls, and
the boys knew exactly what they were going to do for the
next few years.

"Remember me?" asked one I didn't remember. "I was
about to start at the *Instituto*. Well, I have decided I am
going to be a doctor!"

They discussed the movie *Lucia*, of course; how Cubans
don't take army discipline well; the American plane that
had been forced to fly to Havana that day; the book by
Miguel Barnet *The Autobiography of a Runaway Slave*
(published in the U.S. two years ago) and, apropos of it,
their pleasure that modern books reproduced speech realis-
tically. But never, as happens with people in their late twen-

ties and thirties, did they pause to wonder at how the revolution had changed things. When I commented on this, one said, "Maybe it is because we are living the revolution."

I was lucky, therefore, to find, when I returned to Havana, a girl in their age group (seventeen) who because of special circumstances was more self-conscious about how the revolution affected her. Celia was born in New York of Cuban parents who had left long before the revolution, and although they had returned every year, her mother and she did not come back for good until 1964. Her mother was a stage designer who worked in the off-Broadway theater, and they lived close to that special hub in Greenwich Village where MacDougal and Bleecker Streets intersect. When I talked to her, her best friend was along, a Young Communist named Marta who attended the same high school as Celia.

"When I came in 1964 I was full of enthusiasm I had picked up on other trips after the revolution," Celia began. "I had wanted to be a Pioneer and now a Young Communist. There wasn't anything I wouldn't do and I felt that way for at least two years. Now I have a lot of criticisms, just as Marta has too, though there are things we disagree about and we argue about them. One of them being voluntary work—"

"You are wrong about that," said Marta.

"You put all those girls together in a barracks and you can't imagine how insupportable it becomes in a week's time. I liked it as an experience the first time but no more —unless they change their strict way of running things. If it were done with some freedom—as in the Isle of Pines where once your day's work is done you can lead your own life—it would be different. But no, restrictions and supervision—it is all extremism. I can't stand extremism of any kind."

The one extremist they both agree about is their school principal, a disciplinarian of the old kind. She once marched Celia and a friend into her school office and temporarily suspended them because she found them— "Imagine, I'm seventeen!"—smoking in the park across the street. Marta said that even the Young Communists had taken up the problem in their organization but nothing had been done. "One of the reasons I am so restive is probably adolescence, I know that," Celia said. "I can't stand rules and exhortations and all that. Everyone feels the same—it doesn't mean we're not serious students, but we're young, after all, and we also want to enjoy ourselves." Marta nodded.

Both had friends among the kids who used to hang around the Rampa, not the hard-core Hippies but certainly those who shared some of their ideology about work and clothes. Yet both are agreed that the Hippies should have been rounded up. Marta was picked up that night. "I really learned about them then," she said. "The obscenities they talked, the hatred of the revolution they expressed, all that upset me terribly. In the room at the police station where they put us two women made love openly and another girl kept telling me that she was bisexual and did not care whom she slept with. When they called us in and I showed my identification card—that I was a Young Communist—they let me go and asked me no questions."

For all that, Celia still feels that the good in the revolution outweighs the bad. "And I am not comparing my school with P.S. 3 in the Village—how I had to maneuver with the Italian and Puerto Rican gangs in order to be safe! Maybe someday I shall feel I have to leave Cuba—I give no guarantees—but for now I am satisfied to remain here."

Celia's mother had listened placidly throughout, and I got up to leave because it was getting toward dinner time. I had learned not to accept dinner invitations: I might unwittingly eat their week's ration of meat. I gave as excuse that I was due to meet the young singer-composers of *Canción Protesta* and mentioned that Silvio Rodriguez would be there. The girls sighed, much as a girl of my generation would have, years ago, if I had told her I'd be seeing Frank Sinatra.

The activities of this group of folksingers emerged from a radio program that Estela Bravo, an American girl married to an Argentinian who has settled in Cuba, conducted on Havana radio. Two years ago she organized a visit to Cuba by folksingers from various countries, and the title of *Canción Protesta* given to that conclave has stuck. Under the sponsorship of Casa de las Americas, a cultural organization headed by Haydee Santamaria, a heroine of the fight against Batista, *Canción Protesta* is now devoted to young singers whom Estela Bravo has discovered; they have an hour television program every month and, at no charge, fill dates at all sorts of gatherings. At Casa de las Americas one evening I ran into an Army transport group who'd come to take them to their base outside Havana, and Mrs. Bravo promised to get them together for me another time.

The other time was in her living room. They were there with their girls and wives and three guitars. Perhaps the most popular with the public at the moment is Silvio Rodriguez, who is twenty-one and has never studied music. He has written some two hundred songs, remembers one hundred well enough to sing them at will, and when he speaks of an old song of his is apt to mean one written four months ago. I told him someone on the bus I had taken to the place was whistling *La Era*, the song I first heard on the school bus in the Isle of Pines, and he said, "I am so sick of it!" He meant it—there was nothing showbiz about any of the young people in the room— because it was the song he'd written the night before which interested him now; one entitled "How Like a Child Is a Boat in the Ocean."

I'd heard that he'd given up the rights to his songs, and he confirmed it. "I do not think music belongs to anyone but to all. I do not want any more money than my television salary. I do not need anymore. . . . I do want to study music, for I am limited by my lack of knowledge. What happens is that I write a certain type of song and then I want to move on and cannot write anymore. Fifteen days will go by and then, unexpectedly, I write something new and I am off again on a series. If I knew more music, I do not think I would go through those terrible periods."

He comes from San Antonio de los Baños, a small town near Havana, and no one in his family is musical. While doing his military service he bought himself a guitar and began to teach himself and compose songs. An officer noticed him and introduced him to radio people in Havana when he finished his tour of duty. He appeared on a television show and in two months had his own half-hour program. "I had never sung to a real audience, only to my compañeros. It was quite a sensation to be suddenly there, but I never felt any stage fright."

He sat on the couch in the living room and sang with great ease, and when others sang, he would, at a nod from them, crouch beside them and harmonize for them. *La Era* is the kind of open ballad that Broadway musicals strive for in every first act, to reprise in the second: the one audiences will hum when they leave. Silvio understands its popularity; it is so singable. Its lyrics contain both his faults ("my metaphors are vague") and his virtues, a warmth of feeling and social concern that, in other songs, lead him and his colleagues to be moral critics. Roughly translated, its chorus follows:

> Our time is giving birth to a heart,
> it can hold out no more, it dies of pain,
> and we must run to help
> for on it our future hangs.
> For any forest in the world, for any street
> I must leave my home and armchair.
> The mother lives until the sun is dead,
> and if it is necessary for life
> we must burn even the sky . . .
> for any man in the world,
> for any street.

The emotional extravagance of the lyrics—their corniness—is more pronounced in English, but there is enough in the Spanish to bother him. His newer lyrics are both more poetical and more precise, and often, as in one called *Paper Smiles*, are bitter comments on moral behavior that has survived under the revolution. I asked him if he had ever had any trouble with his songs for political reasons, if he had been falsely accused, as some poets and writers at that moment were, of being counterrevolutionary.

"I would not permit that," he said, with a rush of emotion that indicated he believed there might be some people in power who might so characterize some of his songs and those of his colleagues. "I would demand an explanation or I would bash their faces in, I do not know what I would do." He paused. "What little trouble I have had has been lack of understanding from the old." I asked if his critics were not ideological, then, but simply older people who couldn't stand the young sound. "Oh yes, society will have to develop quite a bit before the differences between generations is overcome."

When no one was looking, he pointed out a young man in the room and whispered that I must make him sing. "He is—I do not know how to put it—the most contemporary of us." The young man's name was Noel Nicola and he did sing three extraordinary songs. The first one was a series of parental admonitions, such as an overprotective mother might deliver, but the music made them sound unfeeling and vindictive, as if the parent were saying, I do not want you to enjoy life. The second, called *December 3 and 4*, follows exactly the entry for those days in Che's *Bolivian Diary*, delivered laconically, recounting in a few short sentences two uneventful days in the guerrilla band's life; except that the final phrase, *hacia la guerra*, which in context means *about war* but can also mean *to war*, is repeated in crescendo and, thus, becomes a moving call to battle. The last song, about a facile, doctrinaire revolutionary, begins, "This morning, first thing in the morning, I ran into a man who is a regular carton of ideas."

I asked, "Do you sing this to young people? Do they like it?"

Noel was too modest to answer the second question, so Silvio answered for him, "They love it."

"And do they understand what it says?"

The room full of young people laughed and called, "Yes, yes! They understand—we all understand!"

This was my last night in Havana before the final trip to the interior, and it seemed appropriate that I should have spent it with the most sophisticated group of young revolutionaries I had met; young people whose ideal was Che Guevara, known for his truth-telling and moral purity. As appropriate as finding young people during the next three days in Camaguey who were the most disinterested and unquestioning supporters of the daily tasks of the revolution; they were part of the forty thousand who had volunteered for *La Columna Juveníl del Centenario* (The Centennial Youth Column, so named because the first uprising against the Spanish occurred in 1868) to work for two years in the countryside in Camaguey at whatever tasks were set them. They live under quasi-military discipline, and in their barracks there was always one bulletin board, arranged by themselves, devoted to Che: he too was their inspirational example.

It was the army that first proposed the project and that gave it its start by temporarily transferring there some forty thousand recruits, now replaced by as many young men and women civilians. Several times a week city people all over Cuba go to their surrounding fields to cultivate crops that will help feed themselves, but it is to the *Columna* that the country looks to bring them out of their rationing, so that their basic production can still go to export. "Why are you here?" I asked innumerable young people in the *Columna*, trying to make my question sound as personal and practical as possible, and always the answer was, "Because the revolution needs me," not boastfully, not like automatons, but in the sweet, self-deprecating manner of the Cuban campesino.

They were very much like the young people in the Isle of Pines, except that they were not colonizers, that unlike them they were not given a place for which to root, no cities to build and settle in: they were the landless proletariat of communism working in agriculture. Battalion 92 of Division 5, some twenty miles away from the city of Camaguey, had been moved several times since it was organized, and for the last month they had been cutting cane in La Matilde for a small sugar mill nearby. By Christmas the sugar mill would have completed its plan (whereas in previous years milling seldom started before the new year) and the battalion did not know if it would be leaving the camps where they lived (clean, orderly, even landscaped in that one month) for other fields. It did not seem to worry them.

The camps all consisted of dormitories with double-decker bunks close together with only a duffle bag in between for storing clothes; a clean, decorated mess hall; outdoor showers and toilets with large water tanks hovering over them; playing fields and flower beds; a headquarters building where a huge blackboard contained production statistics on a daily basis comparing performance to plan. "Some camps are better," a *politico* of one company said; *politicos* are those in charge of "revolutionary orientation." "Others worse, they sleep in hammocks." The blackboard contained a section on attendance, and one column listed "deserters"; anyone gone more than fifteen days without permission. "Even if they return, we do not change the records," the *politico* explained. "We are not interested in punishment, we write to them and talk to them and try to find out what is wrong."

From one bulletin board I copied down the punishments meted out, in ascending scale, to those who break rules: (1) private warning, (2) public criticism, (3) suspension of Sunday leave for no more than three months, (4) temporary loss of "honors," such as being avant garde workers, (5) transfer to a company composed of other discipline problems, and, worst of all, (6) expulsion from the *Columna*.

Battalion 92's camps have no electricity, so the work schedule is arranged to allow for classes in the middle of the day. (No project is planned in Cuba without provision for study.) By six in the morning the companies are up and at six-thirty are out in the fields cutting cane; around nine there is a break for a bite, like bread and soda pop; from noon to three, lunch and classes; at six they return to battalion headquarters' parade grounds to hear the results of the day's production; then to their separate camps for showers, dinner, and bed by ten. They travel between these places in the trucks and wagons that also cart away the cane to the sugar mill, all standing and jammed together and—too corny for anyone who has not seen them to believe—singing.

I was walking around the camps for Companies 1 and 2 when they came in for lunch, and took a metal tray and joined them: beans and rice, meat stew (from canned Soviet beef), bread, candied papaya, and coffee. I learned the other companies were too far from their camps to return at lunch, so I got into a jeep to join them. The first, Company 5, had eaten the same lunch and were now stretched under a wagon while one of their teachers filled out cards to organize the transport to take them home for Christmas holidays. The teachers, young men with at least junior high school training who had taken a special forty-five-day course that summer in Havana, worked with them in the fields in the morning; after classes they re-

turned to camp to correct that day's work and prepare the
next day's class programs.

When they learned I was not Cuban, they crowded
around me, each holding his own machete, and began to
teach me how to swing it, how to stand when doing so,
how to remove the leaves from the cane stalk with one
stroke. They also loved to have their photograph taken,
and when I reloaded the camera, the entire company
stood round me, fascinated, as Cubans usually are, by any
mechanical process. There was much banter, much kidding, but all became quiet and serious when they broke
up into three groups for their classes, right there in the
open field.

It was my turn then to be surprised: one class was at
second-grade level, the other third, and the most advanced at fifth. They were mature young men, but for
their hour and forty minutes of classes they turned into
young children. Their concentration was both awesome
and heart-breaking: a young man with a wife and child
back home stands up holding a primer textbook entitled
I Know How to Read and reads aloud that day's assign-
ment printed in 12-point type, haltingly, as if his honor
depended on it: "In Cuba today there are many mines."
It comes out perfect, but the title of the paragraph—"Min-
erals"—is a four-syllable word in Spanish and he does not
get it right the first time.

When he finished, the teacher asked, "What is an
archipelago?" and I moved on to the third-grade class
where with a gasoline drum top as blackboard they were
learning a vocabulary list and separating each word into
syllables. (Later I learned they have portable black-
boards in their camp and had forgotten to bring them to
the field that day.) In the fifth grade, they had begun

with math and by the time I joined them were doing
Spanish; their teacher asked them to write a slogan for
Viet Nam, and for five minutes each worked silently in his
notebook. Each slogan was read aloud, its grammar corrected, and the class voted for one to be put up at their
camp's bulletin board: "Viet Nam, imperialism will fail because you battle for a just cause." The winner stayed at
the wagon for a couple of minutes to copy it out in ink
while the rest of the company headed for the standing
cane for another three hours.

When they returned to battalion headquarters at six-
thirty, I was talking to the battalion commander, a Negro
captain who had fought in the Sierra Maestra. He heard
them singing and smiled as a reflex. I asked him if young
people in his hometown of Bayamo had been very different
in his time from these boys about to parade for us and
discuss with him the day's production. "Night and day!" the
captain said. "When I think of myself at their age—I had
already gotten two or three doses of clap from fooling
around. These boys are so innocent and sound—they are
so *good.*"

The day with Battalion 92 had been impressive, but I
remembered a moment at the end of my first week that
had told me more about what had happened to young
people under the revolution. Perhaps because, obliquely,
it had involved me personally. I was in the airport at the
Isle of Pines waiting for my plane, delayed because morning fog had kept it from landing. In the waiting room I
ran into Lilian Tauler, a twenty-six-year-old who worked
in the Party's propaganda section arranging itineraries for
visitors, something she had done for me some days earlier.
She was waiting for North Koreans due on the Havana
plane. Chatting to no purpose, I found out she was from

Holguin, a large city in northern Oriente province, and I asked her if she knew of a rich family there, distant relatives of mine I had visited in 1960, who once had great holdings in sugar cane and real estate and were all now in Spain or the States.

"Oh yes, that great mansion in front of the park," she said. "The street they lived on was named after them. They did not even bother to belong to *El Liceo,* for that was a social organization to which even the Spanish shop-owners could belong. They were members of *El Tenis!* And there was Clarita, just a little older than me, so tall and beautiful." She stopped, and in her inward glance I detected—I was certain of this—her wonder that there could have been a time when she had envied Clarita. Like a movie ending, the loudspeakers announced the arrival of the Havana plane, and the look disappeared from her face. She shook hands and smiled. "I must get on with my job," she said.

III

The Wrinkles
in Carefree Brazil

The flight from New York to Rio de Janeiro is interrupted, a little after six in the morning, by a thirty-minute
stop in Brasilia, and the night's uneasy sleep and no breakfast made the terminal seem no more than an uninviting
shed. Much more dismaying was the first of several posters pasted to windows inside the terminal—though perfectly right for a country that has been ruled by the military
since 1964. Above a block of photographs of several men
and women, it said: "Wanted Terrorists"; below, "They
assault, rob, kill heads of families." Yet three and a half
hours later, the taxi from the Rio airport suddenly entered

the Flamengo section of the city and that extraordinarily beautiful vista of mountains and beaches surrounding a modern city, so familiar from photographs, totally dispelled the grim first impression. The sun was out and anyone not shopping or working was already waiting, towel in hand, for a stop light to cross over to the magnificent beaches that stretch along the southern edge of the city and beyond, beaches as accessible to natives as to tourists in the hotels in Copacabana. The only note of tension was supplied by the traffic—exuberant, aggressive, unheedful of rules—but no one minded that but me.

It was the beginning of the last week in September, and since the first a military junta had taken power to keep the vice president, who unlike ailing President Costa e Silva was a civilian, from ruling; the American Ambassador had been kidnapped on the fifth and released only when fifteen political prisoners were put on a plane to Mexico and a statement by revolutionary groups was published and read on television and radio; assaults on banks that had been going on all year continued; a Government decree announced the death penalty for persons guilty of a subversive act; and rumors placed the number of people rounded up by the secret police that month as high as 1,800. Astonishing that none of this showed in the life of the city, and I said so to a foreign newspaperman the first day. "I tell you, no more than five hundred people in this country care," he said. "They have the beach, they have *futbol.*"

When I left Rio ten days later, the city looked just as gay and unconcerned but I had talked to many people who were not. True, I had purposely come to Brazil to seek out those who were opposed to the military dictatorship and to try to gauge the nature of their opposition;

but you had only to make the slightest comment about the political situation—the populace was waiting daily, without much suspense, to hear what general the junta would select to be their new president—for people to become wary, feign disinterest, or repeat platitudes. I learned not to talk politics in public situations, nor to keep the names and addresses and telephone numbers of people who talked to me; I didn't take their photographs and I promised to blur their identities.

There was one exception—the courageous Senhora Niomar Moniz Sodre Bittencourt, a woman so unused to curbing her speech that she had already been forced two weeks earlier to give up her newspaper, *Correo da Manha*, and was due to stand trial on the charges of being a subversive person and having cast doubt on the honor of the armed forces. My last night in Rio I spent with two members of one of the important underground revolutionary groups, and after I left them, a car backfiring on Copacabana Avenue was enough to make me jump.

Yet the ambience of the city is one that tempts you at every turn to enjoy yourself, and even after I had learned that an undercurrent of fear underlies much of its relaxed, carefree surface, it seemed quite natural to me that many, especially the youth, should have only the beach, bossa nova, and *futbol* on their minds. A young man I met leaving the beach a couple of days after I arrived seemed to me typical of that sensual response. At least, I thought so the first time. I was seated on a bench across from my hotel, looking at the sand and water and waiting for a clandestine contact I had made to walk by, and the young man stopped to wipe sand off his legs before crossing the avenue into the city.

He looked at me and said suddenly in English, "You are

American." He had visited New York and was saving to visit California next year. I asked him, feigning ignorance, if a new president had been selected. "I do not know, I am on vacation, I do not read newspapers." He accompanied each statement with an impatient stroke that got rid of more sand. Then he looked up and smiled. "Who cares about politics? I like to dance, I like the beach—isn't that enough?" He put on his sneakers and started to leave. "Since five o'clock," he called back, after he had walked a few paces, "it is the beginning of spring!"

The next time I saw him he was again just leaving the beach. This afternoon there was a friend with him. "No new president yet?" I said. He shrugged his shoulders exaggeratedly to show he knew I was kidding, but his friend replied, "You understand that we are going to have a new president but no one is going to vote. Only the generals —terrible!"

I nodded, and the carefree young man shrugged again and grimaced and said to both of us, "Oh, don't talk politics."

But once started, his friend could not stop. "Last year, friends of mine—students—were killed, and so when I talk about politics I get very mad. My uncle is a general, and he yells at me when I talk this way. You know what's wrong here—I'm sorry, I forgot you are an American."

I shook my head, indicating he should not spare me, but so many thoughts seemed to be assaulting him at once that he could not respond immediately.

The carefree one raised a hand to get our attention. "Listen, I think we should gather up all the gold in Brazil and take it to Nixon," he argued, forgetting that he hated politics. "And when we hand it to him we say, Here, it's all yours—now leave us alone!"

His friend shook his head slowly, sadly. "That's not funny. This is our country, after all . . ."

The other gave him a friendly push and made a funny face at me. "Come on, let's go," he said, and then struck himself on the forehead. "I *hate* politics!"

The first day I took a taxi up to Santa Teresa, a neighborhood in the hills overlooking the commercial center of the city, no longer as fashionable as Copacabana, which is no longer as fashionable as Ipanema, which is no longer as fashionable as Leblon, all three of which lie along the beaches going south. The taxi driver maneuvering the steep, twisting streets explained that Santa Teresa is not safe at night now. I told this to the graduate student I visited there, and when he began to explain that the taxi driver really meant Santa Teresa was where Ambassador C. Burke Elbrick had been held, his wife got up and put on the record player. She pointed to the open window behind me to explain we might be overheard. From their tiny balcony they showed me the house where the newspapers said he'd been kept. It had been rented by Elena Bocayuva, daughter of a wealthy, conservative family who lived nearby; Elena was now much wanted by the police.

"Most people do not believe he was held there," the Graduate Student said. "For one thing, they do not believe the newspapers. Second, they do not think the revolutionary groups would select a place where any unusual activity would be noticed. But there are quite a few of us here who have reason to believe it is true."

I asked him what this was. He smiled and said no more, but a few days later he told me. Information that cannot be revealed without sending people to jail . . . a problem that dogs anyone reporting on Brazil. One of the reasons newspapermen in Rio have great difficulty finding people

who have been tortured by the army military police—or
the navy's or air force's, for there are some five police
organizations vying for the job of dealing with subversive
persons—is that Government intelligence watches foreign
publications. Everyone knows the round-up methods, the
tortures inflicted, even most of the people taken this
month, but the tortured tend to go into hiding and will
not speak to anyone but friends.

Where to talk to people and when becomes very com-
plicated. In taxis, one uses a code; there was a rumor that
one of the police organizations had placed its agents with
one fleet of taxis, just to eavesdrop. This last was something I used to hear in Madrid, where I was told the cab
drivers were often provocateurs, led passengers into political talk, and then drove them to police headquarters for
questioning. Whether true or not in Rio, the existence of
the rumor was one piece of evidence that it is a totally
repressive state, an example of modern folklore that one
may intellectually question but would be wise not to test.

One evening a group of social workers spent two hours
trying to find a suitable place to talk to me. None were
revolutionaries and none were leading "illegal" or "clandestine" lives, as others I met, but all despised the military
regime and hoped to tell me how it affected their work.
Their job of dealing with the inhabitants of the *favelas*,
the shanty towns that the poor build wherever there is
nonutilized ground, had never been more than to help
them organize themselves into communities; the social
workers had no funds to dispense, no employment or
schools to offer the *favelados*, but they had, nevertheless,
felt useful in the kind of advice they could give. All that
was past. The government was now only interested in
using them to push the *favelados* out of their homes; there

was a campaign underway to get rid of the *favelas* around the middle-class and wealthy sections of the city, and the inhabitants were being recalcitrant. Their discontent seemed confined to this, for the places offered them, unlike the shacks they built, required payment of rent and were so far removed from the menial jobs they held that they were now faced with total destitution.

Where to talk about this was a problem for the social workers. They would not go up to my hotel room, nor sit in the lobby, nor go to a sidewalk cafe or restaurant. We walked the streets while one or the other went to a public phone and called a friend whose home might be free that night. Finally, an upper-middle-class woman in Leblon who had once interested herself in the problems of the *favelados* invited us to her place. When we got to her apartment, she said quickly in Spanish to me, "Wait fifteen minutes before you start talking—my sister-in-law will have left for the theater by then."

"She doesn't know how you feel?" I said.

"She was here for dinner, and we do not talk about these things," our hostess explained. "She is an American. . . ."

In a moment, a blonde American woman came into the living room and greeted us. She spoke perfect Portuguese and did not take me for an American. As soon as she left, I asked, "But have you ever tried talking to her?"

The hostess shrugged. "When the ambassador was kidnapped, she said it was becoming impossible for Americans to live here, so I do not think I should try. . . ."

"Imagine," said one of the social workers. "It is for us that it is becoming impossible—we cannot even talk."

Only the Old Journalist talked expansively in a public place about politics. A group of us sat around him at a cafe in Ipanema, the section where intellectuals prefer to gather. It has something of the relaxed atmosphere that was Greenwich Village's before it became frantic. But then the Old Journalist comes of an old military family, is a personal friend of the three men who make up the junta, lectures at the War College, and on the whole supports the regime. "What do you think of the kidnapping?" he said, and adjusted his ascot and blazer. "I found it wonderfully amusing, and wished we had a little more freedom of the press. I would have written a column entitled 'Ambassadors of the world—unite!' "

He explained that army officers are members of the traditional military families or the sons of the lower middle class outside the big cities who could not afford to send their scions to good schools. "They are full of a terrible innocence and when they come to power are easily corrupted, for they have not known temptation before. Yet they are real patriots—not that I am—and moralists. But moralists of a Victorian cast who are outraged by little things and think that barracks discipline is what the nation needs. Look at Albuquerque Lima." General Albuquerque Lima was one of the three generals being considered for the presidency. "He actually said in public that he could not understand how the church allows nuns to teach girls about sex!"

The Old Journalist hopes for a strong government, is interested in the developments in Peru, where the military also staged a coup but went on to introduce economic reforms, and admires the United States without wishing its form of government for Brazil. He wants Brazil to get out of what he considers the vicious circle of its politics: parliamentary democracy always leads to liberalism and corruption and necessitates the army—"Only the army matters;

the navy and air force are weak nonentities"—stepping in
with its good intentions and narrow views. He is both dismayed by the political situation and pleased by the emer-
gence of a revolutionary urban guerrilla. "Polarization is
good—it clarifies the issues."

He knew I'd spent the previous evening with Left
Liberals who were friends of ex-Presidents Juscelino
Kubitschek and Goulart. "Your friends, the bourgeois na-
tionalists, are powerless. In extreme crises the center atro-
phies, becomes subject to paralysis—they have, thank-
fully, no role to play. What we need is to get Brazil out of
its vicious circle by encouraging the military to listen to
the people. I shall be speaking to some these days and
this is the advice I shall give them." His sense of irony
made him add, "Though they will not ask for it."

The evening I spent with the Left Liberals (these
labels, necessary to preserve anonymity in this report, do
not do them justice, because as individuals they are difficult to fit into a single political stance) was in fashionable
Leblon. A large, comfortable home across from the sea;
on its garden wall the Communists had painted earlier in
the year "Go Home Rocky," "Long Live the Communist
Party." The living room was filled throughout the evening
—friends in Rio drop in on one another without warning
—with professionals and intellectuals. They admit to
powerlessness, and their only hope is based on their belief
that everyone else is unhappy too. "Maybe the best we
can hope for," someone said, "is that the new president
they select gets sick in a month or two and the generals
will have to spend as much time picking another as they
are doing now . . . while the country flounders."

It was not meant seriously, of course, but they do seem
to trust to some degree that the generals will fumble

themselves out of power. "Well, you must admit this is a more democratic selection of a president than the last time," another said. "This time the eight four-star generals are consulting the three-star generals. There are twenty of these, so that widens the base considerably!"

None there believed in guerrilla warfare—urban or countryside—to bring down the government. One went so far as to say it was madness, but the discomfiture of the regime with the Ambassador's kidnapping gave them much pleasure. They enjoyed telling me that when the message of the underground groups was read on prime-time television (a condition for freeing the Ambassador) the regular announcer read it with feeling. No one knew whether it was out of professionalism that he read it this way or because he was pleased with what it said, but some generals were rumored to have wanted his imprisonment. Everyone was nostalgic about that delicious day, though it had only occurred earlier in the month, when the revolutionaries' message had to be printed in all newspapers and read on radio, and everywhere in Rio you could hear people make political comments that had been bottled for so long.

One of the Left Liberals had been in Goulart's entourage when as vice-president he was abroad on a goodwill trip. They were in China when the news reached them that President Quadros had resigned because of pressure from the Right. Someone ordered champagne and proposed a toast to the new president. Goulart would not drink to that. "Let us rather drink to the unforeseeable," he said. And someone turned to me and said, "That is the way it has been ever since in our country—unforeseeable. Except that nowadays the unforeseeable has to be a general."

An intellectual who had spent nine days under arrest that month described the state of the nation succinctly: "In this country the rich are dying of rage and the poor of hunger." By inference, the Intellectual was also saying that the workers were not politically aroused by the country's dictatorship. Certainly the trade unions had long ago been tamed by the removal of their old leaders and the appointment of friends of the regime. However, the greater amount of sabotage and clandestine activity in São Paulo as compared to other cities was always explained by its being an industrial city with a great concentration of politically conscious workers. Yet in the main the resistance to the regime came from the middle class, its professionals, the students, and the increasingly active left wing of the Catholic Church.

At that point someone came in and took the host aside, but the host repeated the news. "The Bocayuva family was released this afternoon." The Intellectual had been at the military police jail with them and he recreated the scene for us: a large anteroom where people sat and filled out a form in which they gave a kind of job résumé of their lives and spelled out just where they had been during the days of the kidnapping. A short corridor led to the room where a sadistic captain and a kind lieutenant conducted the questioning, two soldiers standing by with rifles at the ready and a third holding the electrical gimmick with which they administer shock treatment to the genitals.

I spoke to two persons besides the Intellectual who were in and out of those rooms that month and their descriptions supported one another. All three remembered the gunshots at intervals outside the building, followed by an officer entering the room calling out to a colleague,

"Well, that's two more of them!" Two of these persons I spoke with were offered homosexuals whom the M.P.'s had picked up one evening to spend the night in their cells; one was not. One got to the point during the questioning when the electrical shock was to be applied; two only listened to a description of the tortures. All three were in the anteroom when they heard the agonized screams of a newspaperman and saw him led back to the anteroom, stumbling and shaking, by the lieutenant who played the kindly role.

"But you know, there is great division in the army that has been aggravated by the kidnapping," said the Intellectual. "During my nine days of psychological pressures I had to be accompanied from one place to another in jail frequently. Always by an officer. Finally, I asked one of them why him, for in my days in the army that kind of job was done by a corporal at most. He said that with political prisoners they did not trust enlisted men."

The host interrupted him and said to me, "I wonder if you know that all this—these tortures, the death penalty for subversive acts, the terrorism of the underground groups—is new to our country? We have had coups and coups but they have never involved this."

("Yes, it is true," said the Old Journalist the following evening. "The Brazilian has always solved things through compromise. We have an untranslatable word for that— jeitinho, which is a way of hanging on to things with a combination of skill, greed, astuteness and also dishonesty.")

But someone, I said to the Left Liberals, must be favored by this regime. "Of course, the foreign businesses," said a doctor. "You know the statistics of Dom Helder [the Archbishop of Recife who openly speaks

against the Government] that 50 to 100 percent of each
of our major industries is owned by foreign companies.
The so-called monetary reforms after the coup of '64 help
them—when money gets tight, they have enormous capital to fall back on, but our businessmen fail."

The next morning, between appointments, I shared a
sidewalk table on Avenida Rio Branco in the commercial
center of the city with an Englishman reading the *Econ-
omist*. He was drinking beer and picking at broiled hors
d'oeuvres. A neat man in a tropical country, he gave me a
précis of the situation. "For a fortnight now the military
has been trying to select a new president since the old
one is ill and incapable of carrying on the job. One
doesn't know if he's really ill or if the hard-line generals
were simply dissatisfied with him. No one much cares
really, it has no importance."

We exchanged superior smiles about the natives.

"Of course, there's such a thing as political rights, but I
believe the man in the streets also has rights that should
be respected. These are to go about his business without
student disturbances and dislocations. I'm with the light-
and-power company and we've had no problems. We do
hope that when they select a new man that it shan't be a
hard-liner because then the situation might become like
Argentina's—strikes and shootings and rebellions. You can
see that the physical dislocations here all come from rapid
development. For ten years we made no new investment
because the Government was so left wing that the situation was untenable. Now we're having to hurry these ten
years into two."

I had just come from a magazine publisher's office and
had time on my hands because he had been unable to talk
that morning. "I *want* to talk to you but I have no chance

today," he had explained. "Two of my editors were arrested yesterday, and this morning I received a call from the army secret police telling me that they still consider me a subversive person. I spent a month in jail earlier this year, and this means I could be picked up any moment. So I'm trying to get everything done to keep the magazine going. If they pick a new president in the next couple of days, I may be in the clear, simply because the authorities will be less nervous. I shall call you, but of course not from this phone—it is tapped."

An hour and a half later I was having a relaxed lunch with a friend of his, a wealthy businessman, in an alcove all our own in a luxurious restaurant in the Swiss Embassy building. The Wealthy Businessman is a left-wing nationalist, and he is no more popular with the regime than the Magazine Publisher. But his wealth—and also his charm —create deference wherever he goes and if the waiters overheard what he was saying, they did not show it. He talked about his good friend, José Emirio de Moraes, Brazil's richest man. "He is in textile, steel, aluminum, cement, paper, chemicals—he has built up enormous businesses but he has had to do it fighting the foreign firms every step of the way. When he went into steel, that light-and-power company for whom your English friend works almost stopped him, but he built his own power plant to supply the electricity they denied him."

He took a clipping from his wallet. "This is what José Emirio said when he heard a foreign company was given preferential terms to invest in Brazil." He gave me a clipping that said: "Instead of bringing in a bull that will produce, they have found a calf that sucks."

"Only the other day an executive of the light-and-power company refused my firm a ten-day credit extension, an

ordinary request normally honored without question. He
let it be known that he refused because he did not like my
opinions about what is happening in my country." The
Wealthy Businessman paused a moment. "That hurts me
—I am a Brazilian, he is English."

"When Bobby Kennedy came to Brazil, he took time to
meet with a group of us. But he brought along as adviser
a man who I understand now writes a great deal about
Latin American affairs. The adviser explained away everything we said, and I particularly angered him when I told
Mr. Kennedy that foreign companies have always been
the recipients of your foreign aid. His adviser challenged
me, so I pointed out that our state-owned oil company had
for a long time applied for a development loan with no
success. The man simply yelled that I lied. That is the
way it is."

There is—the Old Journalist was right—a deep frustra-
tion and despair in these men who, left-wing as they
might seem in the United States, do constitute Brazil's
center. They are the people who want to find, as they say,
"a political solution" to the dictatorship. (Curiously, "they"
includes the orthodox Communists.) They would like to
see the country return to constitutional democracy and to
institute wide social and economic reforms while maintaining a mixed economy. The clandestine movement,
however, wants socialism, and the very nature of its tactics is a call to the left to abandon reformism and return
to the Leninist logic of revolution.

All that sustains these Brazilian democrats is their sense
of humor. At the home of the Wealthy Businessman one
evening, many of the guests were men who have been
deprived, by government decree, of every political right
since the 1964 coup, and they played the game, over

coffee and brandy, of calculating how many political prisoners would have been as readily freed by the military regime if some ambassador other than ours had been kidnapped. They decided that Haiti's ranked lowest; he'd have to be taken twice to effect the release of one prisoner. What an escape from the oppressiveness of the regime their laughter afforded them! They were all successful men by any standard—academicians of all disciplines or bureaucrats and politicians who had come to their former positions in government with solid achievements in other fields—and their lives, if not their comforts, seemed canceled by the stupefying ambience the militarists created.

I shouldn't qualify that last statement, for some had been in jail and others of their milieu were in exile. For example, the Magazine Publisher walked in with his wife after dinner, and we greeted one another like old friends. I clapped him on the back, glad that he had not been arrested. For a second, it occurred to me I should not have made even an oblique reference to that possibility in front of his wife. She sensed what had gone through my mind, and said, "We no longer worry about a thing until it happens. When they took him off to jail the last time, he wrote long instructions for me in case he got killed. In those days some political prisoners, it was thought, were put on a plane and then dumped at sea. So. . . ." And she made a gesture that was expressive of a host of things: that it was no use overreacting, that others were going through worse experiences, that it was for everyone there something of a common condition.

Yet I could not entirely put out of my mind the spaciousness and richness of the sitting rooms in that home, the quality of the crystal that held the finest of brandies, and the manner of those charming people that showed no consciousness of the things that jarred me. The dinner had been informal—my host had called to make sure I didn't bother with a tie and jacket—and the cross-conversations many and lively, the laughter frequent and unrestrained. Those who were not expected until after dinner but arrived early drew up chairs and joined the talk. The women serving were completely correct and impersonal, and wore matching black and white uniforms. They were small, dark, thin women, their physique of the kind that generations of undernourishment produces in Latin countires. No one addressed them or looked their way. They seemed to require no directions from the hostess. One or another was at my side with the heavy silver trays as soon as I finished any part of my dish, so thoughtfully that I glanced up the first time it occurred, smiled, and thanked her. She did not acknowledge this, and her look was as unswerving as a soldier's at attention. Throughout the meal they were indefatigable, but their faces remained so closed that the emotion they projected was akin to anger.

When I had arrived at the house, I noticed, as soon as I stepped out of my taxi, the silhouette of a man watching me from a knoll on the grounds. There was something about his stance—it was too dark to see him clearly—that suggested a soldier, and as I turned to the walk leading to the house, he came nearer, and I saw he wore a uniform. At that moment the door opened, and my host stood in the light with a welcoming smile, but I had already experienced a thrill of fear. During the evening, the outline of the guard's figure could be seen parading past the long windows and glass walls of the rooms we moved in. I was never really certain that he was not a military policeman placed on the Wealthy Businessman's grounds by the regime. When I left he was again on the front walk, standing stiffly, his arms at his side, and I decided to ask my host who he was. The wrong question; it embarrassed him. "There are favelas nearby," he said. "My wife . . . this way her mind is at ease during the time I must be away from home. . . ."

I left the dinner party early to keep an appointment with a young man of the extreme Left who for almost a year has been leading a life that is illegal, as he puts it, but not clandestine. I had known him for four days and had been arguing with him about the nationalist bourgeoisie. "Now that you have seen them in that rich home which is their natural setting," he said that night, "do you expect anything from them?"

How does anyone on a quick visit meet such a young man who can lead you as he did me, to a meeting with one of the important new underground groups responsible for the holdups and the kidnapping—people who are the object of the police search going on? An American academician whose father was an exiled Spanish Republican remembered that his father's life was saved by people who hid him during the Nazi occupation, and so the academician hid this young man last year when he spent his sabbatical in Rio. The young man has been moving from one place to another since; he asked me to call him Pedro in public, and it was our joke that I called him Dom Pedro after Brazil's nineteenth-century emperor. We also played another game—that he had no connection with underground groups and that it had been a coincidence that he ran into someone who might interest me. That night he said, "My friends would like to have better proof that you are a person of confidence than the fact that you are a friend of the American professor."

When I asked him what, exactly, he was doing these

days, he said he is now studying on his own, then looked at me and laughed, because he saw I knew he was not being open. "No, I am reading some Marx," he said, "and thinking a great deal about what Che has written." He explained that the period of preparation is something Che mentions but does not expand on, and there are many questions to ponder and discuss; for example, how are the masses to be organized clandestinely? "One thing I know, it is going to be a long fight," he added. "Another, that there is no hope from the nationalist bourgeoisie. Ask them when you see them again what they can do, what influence they can have on the generals, and listen to what they tell you. Economically, they are condemned to picking up small droppings from the imperialists' tables."

Dom Pedro decided to tell me why he was in hiding. In September of 1968 the national leadership of U.N.E. (National Student Union), banned after the '64 coup, decided to call a national congress. Eight hundred members got together at a farm outside São Paulo, were surprised by the army police, and taken in a body to jail. Dom Pedro was one of them. It was in the days before torture became commonplace, and they were released nine days later, to be called again in groups as their trials were due. Dom Pedro decided he would not answer the call when it came, and his group was supposed to be tried that month we met. Some thirty who showed up for trials this year had received jail sentences, while others were denied the right to study at any school or, like Dom Pedro, were in hiding. "That congress was a fiasco," he said, "but it was a good lesson for us."

"The whole experience was a lesson in the weakness of the middle-class mentality—how it can swing from the most radical extremism to ineffectuality. First, we had to argue about whether the congress should be held in secret. The left-wing Catholics and the pro-Chinese wanted it in the open—announcements and all—because in the people is our safety. When, of course, any people's organization to be effective in Brazil these days has to be clandestine. Well, we won and set up a whole security system.

"Why did it fail? First, people were warned not to go into São Paulo itself; but there had been a confrontation between the so-called Death Squad (an unofficial pro-government group of assassins) that is protected by the police and the students of one institute, and the institute was burned to the ground—so some of the delegates decided to go as a gesture of solidarity. Second, four hundred delegates had been elected and eight hundred showed up!"

They spent five days at the farm, it rained all the time, and the congress held only one session before the army came in shooting one morning at seven. "What a miserable crowd they found—cold, sleepy, frightened. The delegates had spent five days huddling from the rain, complaining about the food and sleeping quarters as if it were a picnic they came to, but all the while lobbying for votes before the congress began. The only session we held was spent arguing about who were official delegates with voting rights and who were not. The interesting thing everyone learned was that the soldiers were more scared than we. They did not expect to catch so many, so they had no buses and we all had to march nine miles to the nearest jail."

Dom Pedro shook his head. "The middle class—ah, me! Do you know what they argued about on that nine-mile walk?—whether to tell them proudly what we were all there for. I learned my lesson. I would tell them nothing

and I would not let them catch me again if they let me
go."

Dom Pedro scoffed at me because I planned to have tea
the following day with the wife of a cabinet official in
the Goulart Government now in exile, but he was surprised when next I saw him by what I told him she said.
The maid brought a Georgian silver service to the spa-
cious living room in the Copacabana apartment to which
she had just moved; there were workmen in the rooms beyond, finishing the redecoration. "You may have noticed,"
she said, "that the physical appearance of our city—so
modern and developed at first glance—does not corre-
spond to our people. Some complain that if there is a
pond in a public park it is soon full of debris. Of course,
our people do not know. . . . Why should they know how
to live in the environment when so many are starving?"

She nodded when I told her that a Government econ-
omist had told me that 60 to 70 percent of the people live
outside the economy—are not consumers or producers,
but simply survivors—and that each year almost a million
new workers enter the labor market. "You see these two
men working in my apartment?" she said. "I am inventing
jobs for them to do because there are no others for them
to go to. The minimum salary is $40 a month and for most
workers this minimum salary on which no one can live is
the maximum salary."

She had said that almost everyone was unhappy with
the military Government and that if even a moderately
free election was held they—the military governors—
would all lose their posts. I said that if that were the case
wasn't there some hope that the Brazilian bourgeoisie—I
used Dom Pedro's phrase—would put through the reforms
the country needed. She sighed. "The Brazilian Commu-

nist Party has spent years looking for that progressive bourgeoisie and it has yet to find it."

"Yet on the surface there does not seem to be any crisis," I said.

"Only on the surface," said the Cabinet Official's Wife.

"Only on the surface," said the Protestant Minister of Copacabana, on the last Saturday night of my visit. He and his wife and I were out for the evening, and everywhere the restaurants and theaters were crowded. I had wanted to go to a session of the Festival of Song—the one national event taking place those days that was nonpolitical—but we couldn't make it. The Protestant Minister was just as glad. "This year's festival does not interest us; our best composers have left the country and the organizers are going to make sure nothing happens like last year."

Prior to the repression of December 1968—when congress was dismissed and a wave of arrests took place—there had been a resurgence of political opposition. One unexpected place it surfaced was at the annual festival. During the runoff for the national competition (composers of foreign countries are invited to participate following the selection of the national entry) Geraldo Vandré, a young composer and performer, submitted a number called "Caminhando"—"Walking." It was the great popular favorite and spoke directly about hope and social change. "Come, let us go together now," says the chorus, "for waiting isn't wisdom." It got second prize, but the huge crowd wouldn't let the first prize-winner, an innocuous pop number, be sung until Vandré got up and spoke to the audience. He told them the song wasn't important, that what was important was to do what the song said. Hundreds of people waited for him outside the stadium, linked arms as the song told them, and sang it along with him.

"It was a marvelous evening," said the Protestant Minister's wife.

Geraldo Vandré is now in Europe, and "Caminhando" has long ago been banned. The current favorite is "Aquéle Abraço," and when the authorities gather the meaning of its Aesopian language, it will no doubt also be banned. Without a key, the lyrics and gay music make it seem an affectionate tribute to Rio, a kind of "Give My Regards to Broadway" song; an *abraço*—an embrace—is the way Latins greet one another, and throughout the song Gilberto Gil, the song's composer, sends embraces to the different neighborhoods of Rio.

"Oh, Rio de Janeiro is still beautiful," says the song. "Oh, Rio de Janeiro, February and March!" Just a play on words but most people know that Gil spent February and March in jail. The song then goes on to report how Chacrinha, a popular burlesque comedian, is still repeating his old act—"buzzing the girls, ordering the masses around . . . Chacrinha, that old warrior, that old clown"— and since everyone and every place mentioned receives an embrace but Chacrinha, you know the Chacrinha of the song is any general ruling Rio.

Gilberto Gil also had to leave the country but I heard his song that Saturday night at a show the Protestant Minister picked out at the last moment. It was an evening of songs by Elis Regina, a girl who is at home with an American pop tune, a French song, or a Brazilian samba. When she sang "Aquéle Abraço," she changed the next-to-last line. "Hello, hello, Gilberto Gil—*aquéle abraço!*" and the audience for the first time interrupted her in the midst of a song, applauding furiously.

At a cafe later, the Protestant Minister said, "Would you have known, if you were not in on the secret, what that moment of applause meant?"

I shook my head, and asked him what his sermon to-morrow would be on. I knew that five years of military dictatorship had made him lose his faith. "I am going to speak on the Sermon on the Mount," he said, "but I am going to use Paul Tillich's commentary that dispenses with mysticism and deals with the Sermon on the Mount as Christ explaining social issues to the people of his day."

While waiting for the underground to make up its mind about me and for a friend to reach Senhora Bittencourt, I spent Sunday with an American, Harry Jenkins, whose Southwestern accent made him sound so out of place in Brazil that it was difficult to accept his disclaimer, "Hell, no, man, I'm a Brazilian. Why, I haven't been back to the States in years." Jenkins was born in Brazil, the son of a Methodist missionary, and he was in Rio for a long week-end to see a daughter attending the university. He has spent most of his life in the Northeast, one of the most impoverished areas of the country, working as a contractor, but he knew Rio well enough to take me up and down the surrounding hills and mountains for spectacular views of the city and shore.

On the highest peak in the area, Corcovada, there is a huge statue of Christ with outspread arms. The Ambassador's wife was quoted in a Brazilian newspaper as saying that she knew things would turn out all right because they lived below this statue. "Oh, man," Jenkins said to that. I told him the joke in Rio about the kidnapping that gave one the choice of three fabricated explanations for the Ambassador's moving about the city without a guard: one, the Ambassador had a mistress and did not want anyone but his Portuguese chauffeur to know; two, his chauffeur was his lover and that was the only time they could be alone; three, the Ambassador was stupid. Jenkins opted for the last.

Jenkins had found when he got to the city that his
daughter was one of the hundreds of university students
who during the last few months have been expelled and
not allowed to study anywhere for three years. She was
also in hiding, like Dom Pedro. "A hell of a note," Jenkins
said. He'd introduced her earlier to me but she wouldn't
talk then, nor would she come with us; she wanted to get
some students from the Institute of Social Sciences so they
could speak to me collectively, as it were.

"Damned kids, they think they know everything," Jenkins said.

"Do you have many arguments?" I asked.

Jenkins burst into laughter. "Fact is, they're right. That's
all they can do, the armed struggle. All those liberal businessmen, they don't live the way they talk, so the kids
have to figure it out another way." He laughed again, surprised to be talking this way, and took us down to the
city where, he hoped, the kids were waiting for us.

They had forty-five minutes and wanted to say only
what they thought important. They weren't interested in
questions from me. Jenkins' daughter introduced their
spokesman, a sweet girl of nineteen.

"The Institute of Social Sciences had a small enroll-
ment," she began, "but because of the nature of those three
hundred students it has been the most militant. Let me tell
you. The struggle began after December when the
student-government office was locked by the dean. He
was following the order of the new decree canceling
student-government activities. We met outside and decided to take action. We broke the lock and put up posters and met there. They replaced the lock with a chain,
so we took the door off altogether. We held meetings, put
up posters throughout the school, and issued leaflets. The
school was closed down, some fifty of us were expelled.

We met outside again and decided on a symbolic take-over. We prepared well—lookouts in the streets, a group to call up all the police stations and keep the telephone lines occupied, another squad to plaster the school with posters. After fifteen minutes, we left. No one was caught. But now they ringed the school with barbed wire and kept the school closed while an investigation was done of all the students. Some were taken to jail and when school opened again in June, only 150 of the old students were allowed back."

"Any of you?" I asked.

"Oh, no," one girl said proudly. "We have all been ex-pelled and if we so much as walk by the place we are liable to arrest."

"To get back to the institute," the spokesman said im-patiently. "Once the school opened again, we held another symbolic takeover. At night this time. We used the same tactics, plus one squad to cut a hole through the barbed wire. The police got there while we were still putting up posters—this time we destroyed everything, everything in the dean's office—but we got out through the hole in the barbed wire."

"Now what?" I said.

"Now the school is run with military police walking around in civilian clothes. There is no discussion of any-thing vital in any class. One of the gorillas walked into a class where the professor was discussing the Freudian con-cept of repression and the professor was dismissed. A girl was taken into one of the school offices this week by the police and disrobed and practically raped right there. She has suffered a terrible trauma. We want you to tell that."

Jenkins's daughter looked at her watch. "Go over it," she said.

The sweet girl who had been the spokesman counted off on her fingers the things she wanted me to write. "Remember, they are torturing and jailing students, there is total lack of freedom of expression or avenue for change, armed struggle is the only way to end this. And please say that the president of U.N.E., our national student organization, was badly tortured. They used the telephone [two suction cups clapped simultaneously over the ears] and he may never hear again."

They got up together and before they shook hands the spokesman smiled shyly and said, "And because so many of us must stay away from home unable to work I would like to ask you for a donation."

Jenkins looked over their heads at me and said, "Damned kids."

In a country so anarchically ruled, the new national security law published in full by the newspapers that Sunday read like an admonishment to the entire country. It was both all-inclusively vague and precisely detailed, and covered every possible kind of opposition to the Government short of bad thoughts. One "article" decreed two to six years in jail for anyone offending the honor or dignity of the president or any official down to the state governors, a crime of which a majority of citizens are, no doubt, each day guilty. Senhora Bittencourt had been charged with that and similar crimes with jail terms totaling a minimum of twelve years and a maximum of twenty-two. Her trial was due in a month, but she continued recommitting her offense in public until she had announced two weeks earlier in a front-page editorial of her newspaper that she was resigning as editor because the dictatorship made it impossible to conduct an independent newspaper.

In Rio people loved to tell stories about her, and

whether apocryphal or not they all sounded, once you met her, plausible and probable. Since the dictatorship had announced that it would put an end to corruption, it had made some obeisances to this end by investigating, with a view to eventual trial, private fortunes "illicitly acquired." When Senhora Bittencourt was approached, she said immediately that it was very easy for her to explain her private fortune—her great-grandfather was rich, so were her grandfather, her father, and husband. "I suggest you ask the wife of President Costa e Silva how she acquired her many new dresses and fur coats," she is quoted as saying, "for everyone knows her husband never had more than his general's pay."

She received me for cocktails in the library of her apartment in Flamengo (she has not followed the fashion to Leblon) and in its soft lights she looked extraordinarily young. She was dressed for a dinner party in a short blue dress whose diaphanous sleeves turned into wings as she gestured, reached for the phone, or prepared drinks. "What do you think of the kidnapping?" she, too, began. "I found it very amusing. He was not a good ambassador —he went along with a foolish policy. I was at the press interview he gave. Five days had gone by and he still wore a bandage on his forehead. Like no bandage I have ever seen. There was no bump there, it was all so clean and smooth I felt like ripping it off him. He was a bad ambassador and I do not think all your ambassadors are bad."

She has many friends in the United States, and she and her husband, now dead, were particularly close to Governor Rockefeller. "He always stayed with us when he came to Brazil. It was he who convinced me to start a museum of modern art here. I had a good collection—well, not as

great as some of the private ones in your country, but I
had started buying Monets, Braques, and Soutines at
twenty-two—and Nelson said I had to start a museum.
Because of my appreciation for art and also because of
my privileged position in society. He argued that our having a newspaper was important, too. And that is how I
started the museum in Rio, all through private means, for
the Government never helped directly. It was the first
time that society ladies raised money for culture instead
of charities.

"When Nelson came to Brazil this year, I told your
embassy I would like to see him, but I never heard. I had
asked some ten important people—intelligent, knowledge-
able Brazilians—to help me draw up a paper about the
situation here, so that it would not simply be my opinion
but a consensus. Not a narrative of events either, for I am
certain that Nelson has as good a news-gathering appara-
tus at his disposal as I do. No, it was a paper which contained our judgments and made recommendations."

She shook her head when I asked if Governor Rockefeller replied to it.

"I heard that he appreciated it very much and was
pleased to have it. Also, that he told President Costa e
Silva that when people in the United States heard that
someone like me was jailed—I spent seventy-four days in
jail this year—they were astounded. Costa e Silva replied
that it—my case—was all a matter of politics, nothing
serious. I heard all this from other parties, because from
Nelson I have heard nothing to this day."

I asked her if she couldn't have avoided jail and the
coming trial if she had attacked the dictatorship less
frontally. "Oh, I could not avoid that. It is a matter of
temperament, too; I just do not feel well if I do not say
what I think. Those seventy-four days in jail (thirty in

solitary) were very hard for me. Oh, how I hate monotony and not being able to do things! But it was also good. It strengthened my personality, confirmed me in my beliefs."

I told her that her presence in Brazil must be an embarrassment to the military and they must wish they were rid of her. She laughed, and said that she had been approached with the suggestion she leave; they would give her a passport to go abroad and she would not have to stand trial or face a prison sentence. "I told them I enjoy traveling. I have an apartment in Paris that I do not use frequently enough. But when I go there and for how long and when I return are all matters of my own choosing. I do not do them at anyone's bidding."

She sees only military dictatorships ahead for Latin America and doesn't know how Brazil will get free of its own. She blames the United States a great deal for this situation, citing the profits its industrialists take out of the country, and agreed when I told her the view of young people like Dom Pedro that the Brazilian bourgeoisie was too weak to defend the country's interests. I told her that it was surprising that someone of her class was so close to the Marxists in her interpretation of the problems. "But, of course, Marxism is an objective, intelligent, realistic way of looking at things. I simply do not agree with what it proposes. Not for countries that have developed. It was a solution for Russia and China, yes, but not for us." At the same time she thought the young people in the clandestine movement were splendid. (This, of course, was one of her unexpected contradictory responses, a tribute by a courageous person to others who were also risking their skins; I was to find that the revolutionaries returned the compliment, though they added, like good Marxists, that "she expresses some of the fears and apprehensions of the lower middle class.")

What would she say to them if they were in the room now, knowing what a dangerous course they have taken? "It would be difficult for me to say something to them. I would not tell anyone to stop struggling, even when it means a great sacrifice. I know that it does mean that they will not lead normal lives and that they may not survive to see what their lives would have been. But life does not die out—there will always remain a sediment of what they were."

To Americans she would say: "Follow a more intelligent policy or we shall have Communism all over Latin America of the military kind—a Communism without ideology. Earlier I called it a capitalism without profits but, of course, I do not know of any such thing. American policy is ruinous for us. How? Well, materially—your big companies send home $1.80 for every $2 they make, and you are too accustomed to support dictatorships with whom you can deal easily without all that bother of a congress and president. You should fear them because each dictatorship turns into a menace to you. When a man like Nelson comes here, he should be seeing people of all kinds to find out what everyone feels, and not allow himself to become the prisoner of the Government."

She walked me to the door, and I said that if the military had a good public-relations man they would find a way of not holding the trial and of letting her go free. "I do not know how that can happen," she said. "They have to find me guilty. And hard though prison is I must confess I would feel frustrated if they did not jail me. Jailing me might be a good thing, it might arouse people —and that would be important."

My last night in Rio I met Dom Pedro at the usual corner in Copacabana and we walked several blocks until he asked me to stay put at a sidewalk cafe. I had two demitasses while I waited alone, knowing that they were watching me to see if I was really alone, and when Dom Pedro walked by again, I joined him. He left me at the corner with a young man whom he did not introduce. For good-by, Dom Pedro said, "Give my embrace to the S.D.S." Another young man detached himself from a doorway, and when I suggested dinner, the two led me to a restaurant right on Copacabana Avenue. After we were seated, we looked at one another for the first time, and smiled.

"We are from the V.A.R.-Palmares," one said. "We have been designated to talk to you."

V.A.R.-Palmares (the Armed Revolutionary Vanguard) carries the tag Palmares in honor of the republic set up by runaway slaves, and it is one of the important underground groups, a consolidation of some three armed ones formed this July. These regroupings are part of the process of unification that I had been told was going on. It was not yet well known in Rio that these three groups—one led by the famous Captain Carlos Lamarca who'd deserted the army with a large cache of weapons and ammunition—had now formed a single organization.

"We want you to know first of all," one said, "that we have just begun. We are weak and it is going to be a long struggle. We do not believe in guerrilla struggle alone or in urban guerrillas as opposed to guerrillas in the countryside, but in both plus the organization of the masses of people to make the revolution. It is a long way yet."

Both looked young, but one was thirty and the other twenty-four. Both were former university students. Both led a totally clandestine life, away from family and former friends and haunts. I asked if they knew one another. They smiled. "Only by our assumed names," the older said, and then outlined how their organization functions.

"It is a pyramidal structure, four to six persons to each cell, with one from each being the only contact with the higher one. When a member joins, he is placed in a special group, all of whose members are in the same category as he, and goes through a period of ideological and military training. Not everyone leads a completely clandestine life. There are those who work at regular jobs, lead a seemingly normal life, and then there are those like your friend who is at a halfway stage."

What keeps the principal underground organizations— some four or five—apart, if they all believe in armed struggle? Both a question of strategy and tactics. "The Carlos Marighela group [one of the two that participated in the kidnapping] is purely Debrayist. They pay no attention to the urban proletariat and are only interested in the establishment of guerrilla 'focos.' Also, their militants are diverse, do not follow a single ideological line, and their cells have almost complete autonomy." The VAR-Palmares is critical not only of Régis Debray but also of Che; the former sees the revolutionary struggle as a military operation conducted in the countryside, and the latter never talked of organizing the masses throughout the country. Besides, VAR-Palmares gives only tactical autonomy to each cell; strategy is a democratic decision of the whole organization.

How democratic? I asked.

"Well, we can tell you something that is not yet known —we held a national congress this month. This is why we could not participate in the kidnapping when we were approached one day before it was to occur. We considered that the congress whose plenary sessions were underway had to go on, and we held it throughout this month." They would not tell me where it was held, except that the thirty-two delegates who were elected met as tourists and held separate sessions in groups of eight. Before they met, a military strategy was mapped out in order to escape if they were detected.

"I want you to know," the young one said, "that we approved the kidnapping and consider it well done."

Their faces lighted up when I asked them if they had seen *The Battle of Algiers*. "It is not permitted in Brazil, but we know the scenario." I asked how they could avoid being decimated like the Algerian rebels. "For one thing," one replied, "we dissolve any cell one of whose members have been caught by the authorities—they are to disperse and no one is allowed to contact them—and we have other security measures we cannot tell you about." Then why were fifty-two of their men in jail? "Men caught in holdups were tortured and talked, but all of them were taken before we reorganized in July."

What was decided at the congress? They worked out the line of revolutionary orientation they had described when telling me their differences with Marighela's group; and decided their most important job now was the setting up of guerrilla groups in the countryside, beginning the organization of illegal mass groups, continuing the tactics of bank and business holdups and the theft of weapons from the army. "Also, we shall begin to punish the torturers," said the young one. "Not indiscriminately, but criminals the people know, so they will understand our action."

(Waiting for my plane the next morning I read in the papers that a military policeman in São Paulo was badly wounded by machine-gun fire from a passing car.)

"At the congress, too—and this is not known—it was decided that Lamarca should leave the organization. We will see to it that he has all the means he needs to continue living clandestinely. He is something of a Debrayist and also believes in independent action; he is a very decided man not given to discussing what is to be done with his comrades."

I asked if each cell could decide to hold up a bank. "No, that is one action that is confined to specialized groups. It takes twelve to fifteen men to carry out one holdup and about two weeks of preparation." I had heard that in one of their holdups that month the teller had not only handed over all the money in his cash box but also money a depositor in line had just taken out; the VAR-Palmares men made the teller first enter the depositor's money in the depositor's book. The young one nodded and said, "We give a speech and distribute leaflets if there is time."

The older one volunteered, "We can tell you now that the capture of Ademar de Barros' strongbox was the work of our group." Barros is a former Governor of the State of São Paulo with a reputation for having made his office lucrative, and his strongbox was stolen, some three months after his death last spring, from his mistress' home. The papers carried very little news about it at the time, and the impression left with the public was that it had been full of incriminating documents. "What it really contained was $2,500,000," said the older one with a delighted smile. "I think that is the largest catch any revolutionary group has made anywhere in the world."

"It was known as *la Caixinha de Ademar*," explained the younger one, "after the custom of corrupt bosses who keep a little box on their desks for workers to drop a kickback in."

Two-and-a-half million? I asked.

"In American dollars," said the older one.

How do you live? I asked. "No more than three months in one place." It must mean that you have given up all those things you had—books, records, your own place? "Everything but the books," said the younger one. "I carry those with me like a tortoise his shell."

I shook my head. "You are in this heart and soul?"

They nodded in unison, and the older one grunted for emphasis. "Why—you would not want us to be different?"

I said middle-aged persons with children cannot help but worry about them as children to whom one fears harm may come. They looked at me as if wondering whether someday they too could be subject to such emotions. "It has to be done," the older one said. "There is nothing else to do but this."

We had spent three hours in the restaurant, and we went out on Copacabana Avenue to say good-by. I asked them, as I had Senhora Bittencourt, what they would say to Americans.

"Tell them we are fighting the fight of revolutionaries the world over," said the younger one. "Against imperialism and injustice—"

"Against racial discrimination, as you do," said the older.

"Against poverty," said the younger.

"And the ghettos in the cities," said the older.

"Yes, that too. Against that whole unknown planet that Norman Mailer said no one has wanted to send a spacecraft to. That is the planet we want to liberate."

There was nothing unusual on Copacabana Avenue about three Latins embracing to say good-by. They walked in the direction away from mine, toward their unknown planet.

IV
Chile's
Two Left Wings

The Argentine sociologist who met me at the airport in Santiago knew I was arriving from Brazil, where people were loath to talk politics because of the dictatorship. "No problems like that in Chile," he said. "The whole country is engaged in a kind of political striptease." It was October —spring below the equator—and the presidential candidates for next September's elections had already sprouted, as varied as the wild flowers blooming everywhere. To many, it was all politics as usual—the Right and the Left engaging in fancy footwork before taking their traditional stances behind one candidate—but to others different developments seemed in the offing. It was altogether possible that with new adherents the Left might win this year's elections and begin the peaceful implementation of socialism in Chile.

In 1964, President Eduardo Frei was the candidate of the Christian Democratic Party, and centrists and rightists put forward no candidate and swallowed their dislike of the social reform program of the Christian Democrats in order to make certain that Socialist Salvador Allende, who was backed by other parties of the Left, did not win. The Christian Democrats won by an absolute majority, the first time any party had done so in many years, but conservatives have, in the last five, been alienated by some liberal measures, such as the agrarian reform, that Frei has implemented. On the other hand, left-wing Christian Democrats consider the reforms inadequate to get Chile out of its underdevelopment, and have broken away from the party, promising to back any candidate of the Left if it unites, as it did in 1964, behind one candidate.

There seems little possibility—given these shifts—that the election this year will duplicate the last one. The Christian Democrats will put forward Radomiro Tomic as their candidate; not Frei, because Chilean law does not allow any candidate to succeed himself; and the *Partido Nacional* is urging ex-President Jorge Alessandri, a popular and independent conservative, to run again. "He Shall Return," say the stickers everywhere. All this pleases the Left (besides the left-wing Christian Democrats, they have also won over the Radical Party) because they feel certain that more than one candidate for centrists and conservatives means the Left candidate can win. The five left-wing parties had already announced their candidates by the week prior to my arrival—the most surprising being

the Communist Party's selection of the poet Pablo Neruda
—and were immediately holding meetings at which the
leaders would come to an agreement on which of the five
would become the candidate of the united Left.

There was an almost palpable buoyancy among them,
and it seemed proper to spend my ten days in Santiago
talking to the Left to see close-up what kind of people the
first socialists with the possibility of being voted into
power in the Western hemisphere were like. There were
those on the Left who did not share this confidence—the
students. They were disgusted with elections as a means
of establishing socialism and breaking away from the influence of the United States. Now that it was spring, small
groups of young people went weekends to the mountains
in view of the city to study the terrain and prepare for the
days when they would establish the first guerrilla *foco*.
Armed struggle was their concern. "You cannot win by
rules that others set up," one said to me. The leader of
the Movement of the Revolutionary Left (M.I.R.) told
me at a secretly kept rendezvous—he has been hunted by
the police for several months now—that Chile's one hundred years of bourgeois democracy have left the country
in no better situation than that of Latin American nations
with less respectable forms of government.

Everyone said that these were difficult times economically for Chile, but its problems seemed the continuing
ones of underdevelopment: consumer goods are out of
reach for much of the population; schools and medical
services are inadequate; housing for the poor is miserable; the farmers are without land; and industry cannot
give jobs to those newly arrived on the labor market. Yet
Frei's Agrarian Reform Law, which has given twenty
thousand peasants land, aroused the anger of the Right.

During the international agricultural fair held while I was there, the Minister of Agriculture's speech at the opening ceremonies was interrupted by denunciations from the audience shouted by members of what the newspapers described as the "farm employers' association." Fist fights broke out, and the government issued a counterdenunciation. Two days later a fire spread during the night at the fair and destroyed many of the exhibits, and it was rumored that it might have been the work of the M.I.R.

At a dinner party, a university professor tried to explain Chile's special character. "There are few countries as politicized as ours," he said, his way of saying that all the other nations of the Americas were primitives compared to Chile. There were exiles from Argentina, Brazil, and Uruguay around the table, but he looked at me and added, "You could say that our bourgeois democracy has developed more profoundly than yours."

A woman who was a guidance counselor at the university had little respect for that. "Do you know of a country where even the prostitutes are organized?" she said. "When the Christian Democrats tried to close down the brothels, they sent delegations to see President Frei. They held demostrations, paraded up and down the city. They argued that they protected the virginity of our daughters from the natural impulses of our young men. And they asked the government—Where are the trade schools that are to rehabilitate us?"

"One of the reasons we have developed so differently," said the professor, "is that we are a poor country. We have copper, that is all. There are wealthy families but no great fortunes or a large aristocracy. Chileans are petit-bourgeois and the Left makes a mistake to think that it will ever convince a majority to vote for socialism. They are drawn to reactionaries like Alessandri because when he was president he walked from his apartment to the Presidential Palace every morning and back every afternoon."

"Hasn't someone already pointed out to you the virtues of our flora and fauna?" said the Guidance Counselor, with an ironical smile. Someone had, but I let her continue. "Our climate is moderate and dry, and there are no insects or animals or plants that are poisonous or harmful. Even in our coastal waters, for the cold currents keep sharks away. You can sleep out in the fields without a care. The same with our political life—our radicals do not bite, they conduct election campaigns."

Their most famous radical—without question—is Pablo Neruda, and every newspaper and news broadcast in South America did not fail to carry the announcement three days before I arrived that the Chilean Communist Party, of which he has been a member for many years, had selected him as its candidate. He is, everyone agrees, the greatest poet writing in Spanish, perhaps the finest this century has produced; a literary man in the grand style, an adornment to the nation, Chile's best-known citizen. An invitation to his home at Isla Negra, a lovely beach some two hours from Santiago, is something of a command performance. His home there is a retreat: there are no phones, and to reach him you make a "messenger long-distance call" to Public Telephone No. 1 at Isla Negra. A messenger does, in fact, run to his home and returns with a message or a member of his household.

No one expects that Neruda, now in his middle sixties, will dash to the public phone himself. For one thing, he has gout and moves slowly, but it is also not his style. The opposition newspapers made fun—surprisingly gentle fun—of the idea of his conducting a vigorous campaign. The whole country knows that between three and five he sleeps the siesta, and one columnist wanted to know, should Neruda be elected president, what would happen to the business of the nation during those hours. Others did not take his candidacy seriously, seeing in it a new move of the Communist Party—in the past it supported from the first the candidate proposed by the other left-wing parties—to have a greater say in the selection of a "popular front" candidate. For three presidential campaigns this has always been Allende of the Socialist Party, and one newspaper carried a parody of a poem of Neruda's with the new title of "Please Don't Die, Allende," to make the point that Neruda would be loath not only to campaign for a full year but also to fill the office of president.

Five days after the Communist Party announced his nomination at a press conference where Neruda handled reporters in his magisterial style, I rang the large brass bell at the gate of his home at Isla Negra. Thirty-three years ago, for the equivalent of seventy-five dollars, he bought a tiny house there on some four acres along the shore. There was no electricity or running water then on that uninhabited stretch, but as with Robinson Jeffers at Carmel, civilization has crowded Neruda in. For privacy, he has fenced the entire grounds, so that no one can see from the road, and huge boulders at the water's edge form a natural private cove. A houseboy comes to the gate, lets you wait on the road while he takes your name to Don Pablo, the gate firmly closed again; but when he returns with his master's approval, his welcoming smile is an augury of the warm hospitality that awaits you inside.

The tiny house is no more; there is no house but a series of buildings, mostly of stone, overlooking from high

ground the fabulous shore. An antique railroad engine is
stalled on the lawn, a triangle of brass bells stands ten
feet high between two buildings, and the presidential
candidate waits on the slate walk to greet you with an
ironical, self-deprecating smile. Neruda comes of a poor,
working-class family from the south of Chile, and there
still lurks in his famous, heavy-lidded, aristocratic gaze an
enjoyment of his changed status; it is not constant, but it
does appear at moments like this, when someone who has
known him in another setting first walks into Isla Negra.

Former friends of his had told me I would not find politicians at his home on a Sunday afternooon. Sundays are
his own, just as the siesta hours every afternoon of the
week. True, besides his wife Matilde (famous for the innumerable sonnets and lyrics he has written to her), his
sister, and a niece who take care of him, the only Chileans
there were a couple who were old friends and their grown
children. Yet the other guests made it a public occasion:
Abraham Shlonsky, an important Israeli poet who has
translated Neruda into Hebrew, Shlonsky's wife, and a
young couple from the Israeli embassy to act as interpreters. The guests did not talk politics; the appointment had
been long ago, and the homage to the poet by an Israeli
poet on a goodwill tour must not become a visit to the
Communist politician whose fidelity to the Soviet Union
must place him in opposition to the Israeli government
that waged the six-day war. Try as Neruda did—sitting
behind the bar dispensing drinks, reminiscing about old
friends like Lorca, Eluard, Picasso, whose names are
scrawled on the ceiling's beams—to make it an afternoon
en famille, there were sufficient formal statements via the
interpreters to which Neruda felt obliged to reply in kind
to make the luncheon a diplomatic encounter.

We sat first in the bar—like every room of the place, it had a glass wall fronting the sea—outfitted like a ship's saloon: tables and chairs riveted to the floor, a hand organ in one corner, a wall of glass shelves holding antique bottles, every conceivable brand of liquor behind the bar, funny signs stolen from public bars—a very campy room. Shlonsky mentioned that he first heard Neruda read his poetry in Paris after the war, and Neruda replied that he'd been in exile then. That was a famous period in his life, and I asked him if he really had crossed the Andes disguised as a priest to escape—President Gonzalez Videla had outlawed the Communist Party and Neruda, a Communist Senator then, was liable to imprisonment— and Neruda told the story.

"We had a president here for a while who became a dictator," he explained to Shlonsky, not mentioning Gon-zalez Videla's name, much in the manner of F.D.R., who never named his Republican opponents. "I had written his campaign speeches, worked hard for him—he was the sort of candidate who promised everything to everybody, but it seemed proper to back him then. I did not want— when he turned against us—to go to jail, so I crossed the Andes on horseback. At one point we had to navigate one of those rivers coming down the mountains with a fero-cious current. I feared I would never make it across, and the peasant guiding us called out to me—he knew we were going into deep water—to lift up my legs to the horse's mane. That put me in a position in which the slightest stumbling of the horse would drop me into the current rushing down the mountain, and I do not think I was ever so frightened. I said so when we reached the other side, and the peasant exclaimed, You need not have been afraid for I was right behind you with a lasso ready to catch you. I would not have let anything happen to you, for it was at that very spot that my father once fell and was drowned."

We walked out into the garden so as to be able to enter the building with the round dining room. Another glass wall allowed a view of the sea. A ship's figurehead of Jenny Lind hovered over the dining table—there are several magnificent ones throughout the house, but this was the only American one—and everywhere there were objets d'art collected in Neruda's travels. The food was typically Chilean—a fish done in a delicate tomato sauce with baby shrimps and meat pastries, both dishes that appear in Neruda's poems. For coffee we walked to a formal living room through a passage in whose floor sea shells were imbedded. There were logs burning in the fireplace. Again a glass wall. The objets d'art were uncountable. Don Pablo took out his key ring, opened a door in a stone wall, and asked what liquor we preferred.

One could not help but be struck by the ease of this life, and I asked, "Are you really going to campaign in this election?"

"I have always done it for others," he said, holding with both hands a brilliant cut crystal decanter of gallon size. "This time I shall do it for myself." From the key ring he selected a tiny silver one and inserted it in the lock that opened the silver top of the decanter. "But no more politics, because our friend here is a diplomat and cannot comment."

The young man from the Israeli embassy demurred, and Shlonsky said, "I shall return in six years and see what you have done as president."

"You need not wait so long," Neruda said. "In six months I will have made many changes. Every day Anaconda takes more than one million dollars from our copper mines. Do you know how many schools and hospitals that could build? Between here and Valparaiso—a distance of one hundred kilometers—there is no hospital."

His wife nodded. "One million dollars will build a fine school."

Neruda poured from the enormous, glittering decanter into a tiny glass. "This cognac is only for grand occasions. See how little remains. It is Armenian and of ancient vintage. I forget how many years old it is."

The Hebrew poet was by now a little dazed. When we got up to leave, mindful of Neruda's siesta, Neruda's sister brought us an inscribed copy of each of the two books of poems he had just published, one in Santiago, the other in Buenos Aires. I asked his wife how many editions there were of his books in all languages. She did not know. They kept those books in their bedroom or—she smiled— they would disappear.

"Does all this political activity leave him time to write?" I asked her.

"He has to, he cannot live without it," she said. "If a day goes by that he does not have time to sit at his desk, he becomes very sad, very depressed. He gets ill, so he has to write."

At lunch Neruda had said, "There is a real relationship between a writer and his materials. Writing is also a matter of paper and ink—one has a responsibility to them."

The Argentine sociologist listened impatiently to my description of my afternoon at Isla Negra, and moaned when I told him Neruda was going to take me along on his speaking tour of Santiago in two days. "Very well, I do not deny he is a great poet, but I loathe people like him. Do you know that when he comes to Santiago he stays at the Crillon, our most expensive hotel?"

There are times in Santiago when one believes that the

two major issues that divide the Chilean Left are: one, armed struggle; two, Pablo Neruda's style of living. People are still arguing the pros and cons of his divorce fifteen years ago from his second wife (the first was a Javanese girl he married during his days in consular service) and his marriage immediately afterward to Matilde Urrutia. A young woman for whom all this should have been ancient history turned to me at a dinner party, her eyes alive with indignation, and said, "Do you know that he took *every-thing* when they divorced—even the antique brass door knocker of *her* home—and left her only chipped china!" The presence in Santiago of the second wife, an eighty-year-old woman who is by all accounts an unusual personality, keeps the issue alive.

On a less personal basis, Neruda was at the center, for a while, of the Cubans' critique of the orthodox Latin American parties—and, by simple extension, of their ideological differences with the Soviet Union. That occurred when he attended the P.E.N. International Congress held in New York in 1966. A letter signed by almost every Cuban intellectual accused Neruda of having abetted by his presence the new line of the American ruling class, designed to soften up left-wing Latin Americans. It was the contention of the Cubans that C.I.A.-financed foundations and institutions like the Congress For Cultural Freedom had launched a new offensive in Latin America, one less overtly political since its object was the left-wing intellectuals now so prominent in all fields. The oldtimers, like Victoria Ocampo and Jorge Luis Borges, long the favorites of American attention, were now *"quemados"* (burnt), of no use in reaching a whole new generation, since they were discredited in their eyes by their conservatism and their friendliness to the United States in cold-war days.

Personifying a political line, as the Cubans did by select-
ing Neruda as their target, is risky. Of all the left-wing,
not to say Communist, delegates to the Congress, Neruda
was the only one to speak in a political way, and he had
been very anxious that the Cubans appear, having sent
Alejo Carpentier and Nicolas Guillen a cable as soon as he
arrived and saw they were not there. Nor was there any
question, either, that the flattering reception he received
—particularly at the jammed reading at the Y.M.H.A.—
was in large part due to his being an opponent of our politics. Besides, there were other intellectuals—some on the
editorial board of the Cuban magazine *Casa de las Americas*—at the Congress whose ideological behavior was so
bland that they should have been more castigated—if one
agreed with the Cubans—than Neruda.

The Cubans have tried privately to make up the rup-
ture with Neruda, and although he has publicly reaf-
firmed his support for the Cuban revolution, the attack
still rankles, and he will not accept any of the invitations
the Cubans have since extended him. He had visited
Cuba in 1960 as a guest of the government, and the stories
of his behavior there—all of the antique brass knocker
type—are still current in Santiago. No one forgets. Not
even the Argentine sociologist, who is essentially concerned with the larger issues. The stories are simply too
delicious to abandon entirely, since there always comes a
time in any conversation, no matter how serious the participants, when the question of peaceful transition to socialism as opposed to armed struggle seems abstract and no
longer yields any human interest.

The sociologist's sympathies were reserved for the
young people of the M.I.R. Not that he was convinced
that they could carry through their plans for armed revolt.

For one thing, the preconditions for winning over the Chilean people to so desperate a program were not evident: aside from clashes with workers on strike and with peasants who had seized lands, the most arbitrary recent political act of the government consisted of a presidential decree threatening closure of any publication reporting the activities of the M.I.R. with approval. The editors of *Punto Final,* a political magazine sympathetic to the groups in Latin America waging guerrilla warfare, had been called in and questioned. The photographs of two young men caught in one of the assaults appeared in the newspapers that day, and the sociologist was worried because it was apparent to everyone that they had talked when tortured during their questioning.

"They say this one was so badly treated that his testicles have been destroyed," he said, pointing to one of the photos. "I hid him in my apartment for two weeks once, and I am now wondering how much he talked." He sighed. "This whole question of the use of torture has got to be considered by the revolutionaries. Even in Chile it can happen, and one cannot expect people not to talk when tortured."

Weak and newly arrived as they were, the M.I.R. was forcing Chileans to redefine their political positions. The government and the Right considered them delinquents and outlaws, but there was no popular indignation against them. Certainly the majority of university students in Santiago gave them their approval. My first evening in Santiago I went to a recital of Neruda's poetry at the theater of the College of Music and Arts, hoping to run into him there. A famous Chilean actress did the readings, and the hour—7 P.M.—was perfect for the late dining habits of Chileans. Less than one hundred people showed up. Three hours later the same theater's seats, aisles, and standing room down to the edge of the stage were jammed for the performance of a play about the armed struggle of peasants earlier this century. It was sponsored by the Chilean-Cuban Club in commemoration of the second anniversary of Che Guevara's death, and there was no mistaking the sympathies of the audience who bought every copy of *Granma*, the Cuban newspaper, being sold in the theater.

No mistaking either the effect of the M.I.R. on the university student body. I went out to the College of Education and Philosophy away from the center of the city, its seven thousand undergraduates making it the largest of the state university, and attended a meeting in the auditorium to hear trade union leaders talk about the jailing of factory workers in a recent strike. The officers of the student government holding the meeting were orthodox Young Communists, as were the trade union leaders, and they spoke of lending support to the workers, letting the government know they must be freed. The audience was restive, and one young man jumped to his feet several times to interrupt the bubling rhetoric of the trade union leader. He was the first to be recognized during the question-and-answer period, and he exclaimed, "The same old talk, talk, talk. When are you going to propose some action? Why don't you call a general strike?" He walked out on a wave of applause.

That walkout by a student known to be a Mirista was symbolic of the M.I.R.'s position: the campus is no longer their scene. If they are to make the revolution, they must move away from it, and that is what has already begun. Some sympathetic students complain that this has left them without an organization on campus, and yet the day

I was there the department of sociology was conducting elections for its student officers (the student representatives have a voice in the selection of professors and curriculum) and the M.I.R. group won. The Socialists came in second, the Communists third. The M.I.R. slate had not conducted an active campaign, and the fact that they won gave a lift to the students I was with.

Until then they had been sadly describing what they called the "atomization" of the movement on campus. All in low voices, because they said the campus was now full of police spies. The M.I.R. leaders were not participating in campus politics, but preparing themselves for guerrilla warfare. One of the best known ones, said to have participated in the Bank of London holdup, had entered a hospital gravely ill two days earlier, using an alias, but had had to escape from his bed when recognized. Another wanted by the police was dying in a hospital, and the authorities did not know his identity. "They are wearing themselves out physically," one girl said. "The ones we know here who have gone clandestine all look ill."

The college is as politicized as the nation. Always called *La Pedagogica* (Pedagogic), its new nickname is *La Piedragogica* (*piedra* means stone) because of the many clashes with the police during which the students fling stones from the windows and roofs of the different buildings. Most of its professors are Marxists, and since they and the students elect the administrative officers, the current dean is a Communist. I laughed when the students explained all this, and said, "American students would be happy to have so large a say in their colleges."

"Ah, but *their* problems are different!" said a young sociologist. "They are trying to destroy the universities as an arm of your government. We are fighting to keep ours independent."

They also want to make it possible for others but the middle class to attend. There is no tuition, and there are student loans, but so small that they pay only for carfare— "and maybe a few books," one added—and they must be repaid, without exception, at a figure adjusted to inflationary trends and with interest. There are stiff competitive examinations to enter the university, there being more applicants than facilities for them, and this, plus the fact that working-class families can seldom afford to support their children while going to college, restricts the student body to the lower and upper middle class in the main.

The girl who brought me to the campus knew the United States. "But your universities have such wonderful plants," she said. "Look at our library, totally inadequate. And books here are so expensive, not like your paperbacks."

One young man who had been ruminating spoke up. "But do not let all this politicization fool you—our universities too are an arm of the ruling class."

A collective sigh seemed to emanate from them.

"You are all really for the M.I.R., aren't you?" I said.

"What else is there?" the young man said.

I said that the left-wing parties were confident they could win the elections this time. They laughed. "If they do," said the young man, "they had better be prepared for armed struggle."

I left them for a meeting with Senator Salvador Allende, the man most likely to head the slate of the united Left—the Communist Party, the Socialist Party, the Radical Party, the Social Democratic Party, and the M.A.P.U., the last being a left off-shoot of the Christian Democratic Party. Allende's office in the Senate building is tiny; more than one visitor crowds it, and there were not enough seats in the anteroom to accomodate the peo-

ple who wanted to see him. No one was being turned
back, but he gave me as much time as I wanted, though
he warned me this was not a formal interview. His experience with American journalists, he said, had not been
good, and if I wanted to quote him directly I'd have to
give him written questions to which he'd give me written
replies.

We had met a year earlier in Havana where an elevator
operator at our hotel had introduced us to one another
between the tenth floor and the lobby, and the chat we
had now was as informal—once he told me what he
thought of American newspapers—as that introduction. In
Havana, following the fashion, he had been in shirtsleeves,
but here he was handsomely dressed, in keeping with his
reputation as a man with innumerable suits. He is, however, friendly, talkative, full of eagerness to run for the
presidency for a fourth time, and optimistic about his
chances.

Chileans tired of the traditional parties of. the Left
made as much fun of him as did the conservative newspapers who pictured him as the perennial suitor, but they
respected him more than, say, the Communists. Whereas
the Chilean Communists had only begun to talk well of
Cuba after Castro supported the Soviet invasion of Czechoslovakia, Allende had always defended the Cubans,
even when doing so helped defeat him. I had been told
that he had acted courageously with the five survivors of
Che Guevara's Bolivian group. "He personally went to the
border and escorted them back to Cuba," said the Guidance Counselor who had broken with the Communist
Party six years ago. "He did not leave them for a moment,
because if he did the C.I.A. would have pounced on them.
Those were tense days, and as President of the Senate he
was liable to much criticism, but he did not falter."

I asked him about this, and he told me that he owned a copy of Che Guevara's book on guerrilla warfare that he feels is unique. Che had inscribed it to him, writing that Allende was a man who shared the same goal as he but was going to reach it by another path. When the five guerrillas (three Cubans, two Bolivians) came through Chile, they also signed the same copy of the book. Allende spoke with as much pride about the young men in the M.I.R. Everyone knows that one of its leaders is a nephew of his, a young man married to the daughter of the rector of the Catholic University in Santiago, and he pointed out to me, with a smile, that it was several months now that the police had been searching for his nephew and had yet to find him.

He admitted that he did not agree with their tactics, but he did not volunteer this. He repeated for me what he'd already said to the newspapers: if he were president, these young men would not be fighting clandestinely but working hard to build socialism in Chile.

This reminded me to ask him about his program, and he laughed and said it was the same as his friend Neruda's, with whom he knew I had spent Sunday. The leading conservative newspaper of Santiago, *El Mercurio*, had carried an interview with Neruda in which the poet had given his platform, and Allende referred me to it. It called for the expropriation (without remuneration, except possibly "in some cases") of all foreign and native monopolies, banks and insurance companies, and large industries; and the "deepening" of the agrarian reform begun by the present government. Small farmers and "small and medium capitalists" would be respected, as would freedom of expression and representation for all political parties.

El Mercurio's reporter had gone on to ask Neruda what he would do about the urban guerrillas, and Neruda had

said that he saw no reason to suppose they would continue under his government. Neruda did not stop at this but
added that Communists were opposed to adventurism
and that he did not see who benefited by the actions of
the guerrillas. The Communist newspaper *El Siglo* had on
several occasions criticized them more harshly, and when
I asked Neruda and Volodia Teitelbom, his campaign
manager and a leading Communist Senator, about the
M.I.R., they called its members "the spoiled darlings of
the upper middle class." Both assured me that they were
"totally without contact with the working class," an asser-
tion they made with assurance not only because Miguel
Enriquez, the M.I.R.'s leader, was the son of the rector of
the University of Chile at Concepción but also because at
that moment we were driving to one of the workers'
poblaciones surrounding Santiago to begin his campaign.

To an American the *poblaciones* look like dreadful
shanty towns, but to Chilean workers who were homeless
they are towns they have themselves conquered and built.
Sometimes on their own, sometimes with the help and
direction of the Communist Party, they got together, descended on some large, unoccupied fields, and overnight
built shacks on it and claimed it as their own. Often they
fought the police sent to dispossess them, more often the
government was forced to negotiate peacefully, and lately
the lands are obtained through pressure on the authorities
—petitions, demonstrations, delegations—and the towns
built later. The new *poblaciónes* are swarms from the
older ones, but we were headed for one of the first, called
July 22, a *población* whose lands were seized and fought
for.

It was a weekday morning, and from the dusty streets
came mainly women and old men and many, many chil-

dren. They had decorated the open area where a worn platform served as stage for their gatherings, and the people waiting moved in a mass from our car to the platform that Neruda climbed with difficulty. The women leaders of the *población* greeted him with embraces, and he smiled without a trace of the irony that had always heretofore lingered about his aristocratic eyes. As he was always to do, he spoke extemporaneously, his rhetoric never failing him, and he was never less than himself.

He told them his father was a railroad worker. "I come, then, from the working people, and if I have done something with the poet's life I have led I have done it with the knowledge of where I come from, of the class to which I belong. I know that you are eight years old as a *población*. I am much older—sixty-five—and I have written some forty books, but I would exchange all my life as a poet for that great morning when you took these lands with no other protection than the flag of our country, and built this *población*." They yelled their approval, and he must have noticed during the pause that much of his audience were children not yet of school age, for he added, "If some other candidate saw this scene, he might well say, What votes does this poet hope to gain when there are only children here? But I would answer, I have not come to collect votes but to unite hearts!"

They surrounded him again when he descended the platform, and led him to the *población*'s school. It was new, of brick and polished wood, the classrooms opening onto a center patio, and the children in school uniforms had already gathered in it to hear him. The *población*'s first school had been built by the people themselves. "Just a shack, as you can imagine, sir," a woman standing next to me said, "but we put so much pressure on the government—oh, the number of delegations we sent!—that they gave in and built us this school two years ago, with regular teachers." The principal, a nonpolitical young man, told the children what an honor it was for them to have Pablo Neruda there: "In any country of the world if you speak of Neruda, everyone knows you are speaking of Chile."

When addressing the children, Neruda kept his sentences simpler, but he did not condescend. He told them about the south of Chile and his boyhood there, and spoke of Gabriela Mistral, Chile's Nobel Prize poet, whom he met in those days. "I have taken to the streets now," he said, "not for personal honors but to defend the future of Chile. You will someday see a happy homeland because we are all fighting for it. And perhaps it will be your task to construct that happy homeland." When he finished he walked toward them and they surrounded him, jumping and calling to him, "*Pan de Dios!*"—God's bread, the Chilean's phrase for the Great Good Thing—and the photographer from *El Siglo* went into action.

The photographs blossomed in the pages of the Communist newspaper the next day. Good newspaper copy. At dinner in the home of the Guidance Counselor who hadn't broken with the Communist Party until six years ago, I told the intellectuals there, all people disillusioned with the traditional parties, about my experiences in the different *poblaciones* with Neruda.

"I suppose he had them sing our national anthem?" the Guidance Counselor said. I nodded. "How disgusting!" she exclaimed. "How the Party panders to our ferocious nationalism."

Someone joked that in time the United States would find that it was only the Chilean Communists with whom they could work.

I said there was no denying that the Communist Party was solidly entrenched in the working class.

"Yes, yes, you are right," said the Guidance Counselor. "That is why it is such a wrench to break with it. I still have not gotten over it. . . . You'll see, they will settle on Allende as their candidate, and you will find me working for them again, no matter how little I believe in the whole business."

"Mother, how can you!" said her son, a literature student at the university.

"You must not be so aloof, so skeptical at your age," she said.

"At my age you had certain experiences," he said. "Mine have been different."

It was an old quarrel, so she only shook her head and changed the subject. "But Pablo and I were once very close. He is not this political campaigner nor lord of the manor at Isla Negra—he is bohemian to his very bones."

I argued that this view of him overlooked an enormous number of deeply felt political poems, and that seeing him ignore his painful gout to climb up and down rickety ladders to platforms, walking through public markets chatting and shaking hands, smiling with genuine delight when a crowd of workers pushed toward him—all this convinced me otherwise.

Perhaps what gave them most pause was my account of our running into two old Spanish Republicans while touring with Neruda. After visits to two *poblaciones*, both in a municipality on the outskirts of Santiago, Neruda was given a modest reception at midday in the recreation building overlooking a swimming pool built by the municipal administration whose officers were Communist. They were poor people; one could see that in the food and

drink that they spread out on two long tables, but the
women had gathered wild daisies and placed them along
the edge of the stairs where Neruda was to enter. There
were toasts and jokes and embraces, and of the people
who came up to Neruda two were old men whose accents
were indestructibly Spanish. He listened to them with
special care.

The older one was Asturian, tall, broad-shouldered, big-
featured, and wore a beret as if he had never left home.
He embraced me when he found out I was an American
whose father was born in Spain. He kept an arm over my
shoulder and said, "The United States refused to sell us
arms. I shall not forget that, and I shall not forgive, because if we had had arms I would not be living with the
knowledge that I shall never see my country again." He
had come specially to pay his respects to Neruda. When
the Republic fell, Neruda raised the money and negoti-
ated with both the French and Chilean governments to
rescue three thousand Republican exiles from the concentration camps in southern France.

"Ah yes, the *Winnipeg*," said the Guidance Counselor,
naming the ship Neruda hired to bring them to Chile.

Everyone was silent a moment, and then the Argentine sociologist settled the matter for everyone at the
dinner party. "The fact of the matter is that the Communists here strike me as quite sincere in their reformism," he said, enjoying the irony of it. "They will keep to
their promises, and the parties who form a pact with them
have nothing to fear."

The candidates of the Radical and Social Democratic
parties were out of town during my stay in Santiago, but I
did get to see Jacques Chonchol, the candidate of the
M.A.P.U., the movement which had broken away from

the Christian Democrats and which constituted the one
new element in the coalition. Even those most skeptical of
the respectable electoral tactics of the Left spoke of Chonchol with respect. If the old parties were smart, they
argued, they would nominate Chonchol, who is bright,
unsmirched, Catholic, and quite radical. This was so
widespread an opinion that I was surprised to hear him
say, when we met at his office in the Catholic University,
that he hadn't the slightest hope that the coalition would
settle on him.

So unpolitic a reply destroyed the line of questioning I
had prepared, but I managed to ask him why. "Well, they
are very traditional parties," he said. "I may be too radical for them."

Chonchol heads a research institute which is part of the
Catholic University, devoted to the study of national
problems, and before he became disillusioned with Frei
and the Christian Democrats, worked in the Agrarian Reform program of the government. He is forty-three, looks
younger, and has an unusual background. His degree from
the University of Chile was in agronomy, but he also did
postgraduate work at the London School of Economics
and holds a doctorate in political science from the Sor-
bonne. He worked for F.A.O., an agency of the United
Nations, and as part of this job spent 1961–1962 in Cuba
with I.N.R.A., the Agrarian Reform Institute. He is enthusiastic about the unorthodox way the Cubans have
gone about establishing socialism, and he enjoyed telling
me that American Marxists like Paul Sweezy and the late
Leo Huberman were always puzzled and dismayed by
what they found on their trips to Cuba.

I told him I had certainly been surprised by the Catholic University of Chile—just a quick walk through it

showed that many of its students must favor the M.I.R.;
there were also posters anouncing meetings to honor Che
Guevara—and I asked him if he and the research institute had any problems with the university or the Church.
"None," he said. "We are sponsored by the university."
Knowing the United States, he could imagine the standard I was using for comparison, so he added, "The Church
here is very different. Long before the second council
meeting, it had undergone profound changes."

In his tweed jacket and slacks he looked very much like
a young American university professor, except that he
spoke without the jargon of the academician or the politician. Nor did he avoid problems or contradictions. Unlike other left-wingers he gave Frei credit for trying to
institute reforms. "The Agrarian Reform did give twenty
thousand peasants land," he said, and agreed with the
statement I reported from a Chilean who had been away
the last four years—that whereas there was still poverty
in Chile there was no longer hunger.

Why, then, did he break with the Christian Democrats
and leave his job with the Agrarian Reform program?

"Because there turned out to be forces much stronger
than I expected to the right of Frei and because I saw
that the center, which Frei represents, was not going to
be willing to develop the economy in a socialist context."

Wouldn't the accomplishments of the government work
against the Left coalition in the coming elections?

"No, there is a rhythm of needed change that Frei is
not meeting," he explained. "True, 20,000 peasants received land, but the reform was to have benefited 200,000.
You can imagine how dissatisfied those 180,000 are."

He had spoken so often about the need to develop the
Chilean economy that I said it seemed to me that the

difference between him and the other candidates of the Left was that they saw Chile's need as met by socialism whereas his emphasis was on developing the economy. "No, I mean economic development in a socialist context." He too then spoke of expropriating foreign holdings, with remuneration only if it did not mean sacrificing other plans. "Remuneration or foreign investment in Chile can only be approved on the basis of whether it benefits Chile or not."

I told him that I had heard, even from disinterested foreign observers, that in the election five years ago the propaganda against Allende's sympathy for the Cuban revolution had been conducted on the lowest level. Juana Castro, Fidel's sister, had been invited to tour the country to talk of the evils of the Cuban revolution, and posters everywhere showed Castro sending children off to the Soviet Union or pointing a rifle at helpless old women. How had Chonchol been able to back Frei when such a campaign was conducted?

"We had no control over that," he said. "There was an independent right-wing party which sponsored all that. Frei himself was embarrassed by it. It was disgraceful."

Everyone agrees that such a campaign would scare no one now. The situation has changed in Latin America in the last few years. Both Peru and Chile are talking of re-establishing relations with Cuba. In fact, talk of such a move, as well as the negotiations by the Chilean government to nationalize the copper mines with payment over a period of twenty years, is cited by left-wingers as evidence that the Christian Democrats are thinking of next year's elections in a new way.

I told Chonchol what young people sympathetic to the M.I.R. thought of the attempt to introduce socialism any-

where through elections and asked him what he thought
of the M.I.R.'s program. "I do not think that in Chile we
have reached such a pass," he said. He thought it over
and added, "Not yet."

Whereas Chonchol did not discount the possibility that
violent struggle might some day be necessary, many
others would have agreed with Neruda's statement to me
that "the first to use violence will lose the Chilean people."
Chilean exceptionalism is a popular theme. "In politics,"
the cliché goes, "we Chileans are closer to Europe than to
Latin America." What other country, someone jokingly
asked me, has an airline that reacted to the hijacking as
ours did? That week of the anniversary of Che Guevara's
death one plane originating in Argentina was hijacked
and stopped at Santiago's airport for refueling. Chile's airline issued an announcement a couple of days later that
its pilots were instructed to obey any hijacker's request to
fly to Cuba and that the song *We're Going to Havana*
was to be played immediately on the plane, followed by
other Cuban popular songs; free liquor, candy, and an extra meal were to be distributed, and the passengers promised a sightseeing tour of Havana, also free.

Despite such displays of accommodation to the new tem-
per by the government, there is tension in the air. The
alarmed response to the activities of the urban guerrillas
is one indicator. Inflation and unemployment continue.
"We consume like the most sophisticated country," a
newspaperman said to me, "and produce like a primitive
one." The scarcity of meat makes it unavailable, even in
restaurants, for twelve days each month. "Only the poor
suffer from this rationing," the newspaperman continued.
"They cannot buy in quantities and refrigerate it." While
I was there, the government announced that potatoes

would not be sold for a two-week period. There were signs that Army men were desperately dissatisfied with their low pay, and the Communist newspaper published a sympathetic article about it; some ten days after I left there was an abortive revolt led by a retired general.

If folksingers are a weathervane of how people feel, the M.I.R. has a large potential following in Chile. I went to La Peña de los Parras one evening, and all the songs with any political content or overtones were of this order. A *peña* means a place where folk songs are played, and Los Parras are the son and daughter of Violeta Parra, a great singer and composer, now dead, who is considered one of Chile's great artists. In a ground-floor apartment near the center of the city, her children carry on the tradition four nights a week. You pay a dollar, get a free glass of wine, and sit on low footstools surrounding the singers. It's dark inside, and the couples lean against one another, but they listen reverentially to the songs—not only Chilean ones, but of every Latin American country, so that one comes away with the impression that the whole continent is in close touch and getting ready for the revolution.

Out in the street, where the lights are brighter, I recognized the literature student whose mother decried his skepticism about political involvement. "I told some friends that you were interested in meeting some in the M.I.R.," he said, after taking me aside, "and it may be possible. I shall call you at your hotel."

"Are you sure?" I said.

"Well, it would not be someone being hunted by the police."

"I understand," I said, but I was disappointed. Yet when he called and spoke in English for the first time—

would I be free to meet him in the lobby in a few minutes?—my hopes rose. But he led me to his Volkswagen
parked in front of the hotel on the busiest street in Santiago, and introduced me to a young man in the front seat
—not a good sign. He drove away from the center of the
city, and when he turned off on a side street, the young
man handed me a scarf and told me he trusted me to
blindfold myself. "You are going to meet some one in hiding," he added.

We drove for quite a while, and when the car stopped,
they told me not to remove the blindfold. They took me
by the elbows and told me we were going to cross a street
but did not warn me about the first curb, I surmised, to
test the blindfold. We climbed stairs, stumbled often, and
finally walked into a modern apartment, full of Indian and
modern art, and the first chair I sat in was of inflated
plastic. We looked at one another, and I was told to wait.
Within five minutes four men came into the apartment—
all young—and the oldest told me they could spend only
fifteen minutes and if I had any questions in writing,
they would take them and answer me by mail. One man
went out again to watch for anyone coming up the stairs,
and one stayed at the door inside the apartment; the
others sat facing me.

When I asked, the oldest told me he was Miguel
Enriquez, the other his brother. They took for granted I
knew who they were—the Fidel and Raul Castro of
Chile's urban guerrillas, as some characterized them. Although they finally stayed an hour and a quarter, I could
not get them to talk about themselves as individuals.
"Why," I asked, "did you make this decision, what led
you to take this step?"

"Oh, that is perfectly obvious," Miguel Enriquez replied. "It is a decision that peasants and workers make

every day—there is nothing unusual about it."

He spoke with extraordinary rapidity, but clearly and at length, interrupting himself frequently to ask, "Do I make myself clear?" I attributed this question to his having been a psychiatrist, and to his dead seriousness in being understood. Because I had asked a personal question, he seemed obliged to explain the social origins of all the M.I.R.'s actions. Once, after having underscored that the decision of the M.I.R. to launch an armed struggle was not *voluntarismo* on their part, he asked again if he made himself clear. I answered that I understood they were Marxists, and he relaxed somewhat and indicated to the young man at the door, who for the second time had pointed out that another fifteen minutes had gone by, that he was not ready to leave.

He knew that in Brazil I had spoken to the clandestine movement, and he said that the M.I.R., which had gone clandestine in the last year, was some six months behind the Brazilians. That plus the fact that in any question about the organization of the M.I.R. the words "in transition" showed up in his reply meant to me that they had yet to overcome weaknesses as to security, structure of the organization, and its political line. "We did not mean to be connected to our actions so soon," he said. "We did not want the publicity we have received so soon." And it is true that they have made no claims publicly for any of their actions.

I had heard that the botched-up robbery of a supermarket, where several were caught, had been carried out by a group that had broken off from the M.I.R., and he confirmed this. "What about the Bank of London holdup?" He smiled and said, "You could say some of us were to be found in the neighborhood that day."

Both he and his brother were often subtle in their re-

plies, and they gave an interesting explanation for the
movement's secrecy about their acts of robbery and sabotage. They were not certain that the masses would understand an act like the holdup of a bank, because in so
organized a country—organized, that is, for pragmatic
gains—such an action might seem abstract, difficult to
understand as one done in the masses' behalf. Yet they felt
that people responded better than they had expected: no
indignation on the part of the lower middle class, favor-
able treatment generally by the press, and the obvious
sympathy of ordinary people. "The fact that the fifteen or
twenty of us that the government wants have not yet
been caught is evidence that we have found support."

Since they are so opposed to the electoral tactics of the
Left, I asked them if they were going to do something
about the elections. "Do you mean sabotage?" Miguel answered. "No. We do not think the mass of Chileans would
understand that—not now—and the petit bourgeoisie
might be pushed to the extreme Right."

As with the Brazilians, when I questioned them about
their tactics and strategy in the light of the Cuban experience and the writings and example of Che Guevara, their
almost impatient response could be summed up as, "All
right, we have learned the basic lesson well—armed struggle—but from now on the rest is of our making." They
spoke of the four stages their movement would follow, the
last being a revolutionary war in the cities and countryside, but along the way they would not confine themselves
to military actions alone but work also in the many workers organizations.

Enriquez promised me a copy of their program, and a
mimeographed document of some 150 legal-size pages
was delivered to my hotel the next morning. It gave in

detail not only the principles and program of the M.I.R. but contained an analysis of Chile's problems that constituted an economic and political history of the country. Their position vis-à-vis other left-wing movements was explained, also toward the Soviet Union and the invasion of Czechoslovakia; but the greatest coverage was given to the potentials of a guerrilla movement in Chile. Some of the sections contained a bibliography, citing such sources as Lenin, Trotsky, Althusser, and economic studies sponsored by the United Nations. In that period of preparation which is the first stage of their movement, there seemed to exist no question they had not considered.

I asked if their organization had been affected in the last months since the government has actively begun to suppress them. "We have grown," Enriquez replied. I started to ask how many members they have but began to laugh before I finished the question. "Thousands and thousands," he said, and laughed too.

I told them the Communists considered them the spoiled darlings of the upper middle class, and asked if there were workers in the M.I.R. A bitter smile on his face, he replied, "As to spoiled darlings, the action we have taken has affected our status." His implication was that the reformism of the Communist Party characterized the Communists. "But it is true that there are few workers in our organization. There are a few but not enough yet."

After we had talked about an hour, I commented that they had not, in person or in the articles I had read, inveighed against the United States as much as I had expected. "That is due to the special nature of the domination of our economy. Campesinos and workers do not experience, as Cubans did, the presence of the American exploiters—banks, for example, employ few people, etc.

On a theoretical level imperialism is the primary cause of
our problems, but on the level of political agitation its
character changes."

What would you say to Americans if you were addressing them? "It would depend on which Americans I was
talking to," he said, and everyone laughed. He got up and
extended a hand, and so did his brother. I thanked them
—they had taken a risk in coming to see me—and both
warmed toward me, as if we were all comrades now for
having taken part in a dialogue without betraying one another. "Would you please wait here five minutes after we
leave?" he said. He headed for the door, but returned with
one more request. "I ask you not to give any physical
description."

When they left, the host poured us a drink. We looked
at one another, and I wondered if my eyes shone as theirs
did. I left with the young man whose mother worried
that he was aloof and skeptical. On the stairs he said,
"Isn't he brilliant! He holds all the diverse elements of
the M.I.R. together."

"Why does your mother say you are skeptical?" I asked.

"Well," he said, and paused, loath to say it now. "Perhaps I am because they are too sure of themselves, perhaps
I know what they must think of me for not being one of
them." He paused again, and added, "Though they
trusted me tonight."

That reminded me. "Aren't you going to blindfold me?"

"It is not necessary now," he said. "You did not betray
them when you were on the way to meet them, so you will
not betray them now."

We walked out of a middle-class apartment building,
four blocks from my hotel.

V   Peru's Reformers
in Brass Hats

The Peruvian Army command that in October, 1968, packed President Belaunde off to Argentina says that their rule is a revolution, not an old-style military coup, nor even a temporary intervention in civilian affairs to bring order to the country. Their retirement from every ministry of the government will only come, they say, when the revolution's reforms are irreversible. A few days after the revolution's first anniversary, driving from the airport into Lima I looked for evidence of this: I expected to see slogans painted everywhere and vestiges of the celebrations that must have been held. In Santiago de Chile, from which I had just arrived, you could read the recent political history of the nation on the walls and fences of the city. Not here. On the outskirts, the endless stretches of slums called *jovenes pueblos*—young towns; in the center, the great colonial buildings that the Spaniards erected; everywhere, hordes of people going about their business, with no special elan and certainly none of the euphoria that I found in Havana one year after its revolution. I did not see a single slogan from the airport to my hotel. After ten days, however, I had no doubt that the regime was embarked on a series of projects that is going to keep the army involved in nonmilitary affairs for many years.

It is not unusual, of course, that army generals once in power will not give up their positions quickly—that, in fact, has been the rule in Latin America—but that they should use their power to institute social and economic reforms is new. Six days after they deposed Belaunde and dissolved congress, the new president, General Juan Velasco Alvarado, sent the army to seize the Standard Oil holdings, and last summer he began implementing an agrarian reform law that immediately nationalized the largest sugar cane plantations and mills in the country. Since these are the same army men who in the last six months of 1965 efficiently and ruthlessly squashed the guerrillas whose program included some of the reforms now undertaken, all of Latin America—not to speak of our State Department—has been surprised. "Is it a *real* revolution?" asked the Latin Americans I had met in Brazil and Chile, and this was the question I kept in mind when I talked to people at different levels in the regime—sugar cane workers in the nationalized plantations, wary trade union leaders, left-wing supporters and left-wing critics of the regime, students, independent newspapermen, small businessmen and professionals, and the most famous Peruvian guerrilla leader, Hector Bejar, who has been in jail since 1966.

Perhaps the most dismayed by the Peruvian developments have been the Latin American revolutionaries who for almost a decade now have been convinced that armed struggle to destroy the military and political rulers closely tied to the United States is the only way to bring about basic change. In August, 1969, Fidel Castro made rather friendly statements about the Peruvian regime, and although Latin American revolutionaries have changed and rethought their tactics over the years, especially since the death of Che, Cuba remains the model of what they consider a truly independent, revolutionary government. For them the program of the Peruvian militarists is a tactic of the enemy that has caught them unprepared.

The government has yet to establish relations with Cuba—it is rumored to be in the offing—but throughout its first year it began not only to do so with the Soviet Union and other socialist countries but to exchange commercial delegations. Socialist governments have extended it credit, and when I was there an important group of Soviet technicians arrived to study an irrigation project for which Soviet help was expected. The Peruvians rejected the United States' protest over the seizure of Standard Oil's holdings, and at first it was expected that the Hickenlooper Amendment would be applied to Peru if it did not agree to pay Standard Oil before April of this year. When the time came round, we announced that we would delay indefinitely taking such action. It would have meant Peru's losing its part of the sugar quota and credits under foreign aid.

All these events, everyone feels, are precursors to other,

perhaps equally surprising ones, and the ambience in
Peru, in this sense, is somewhat similar to Cuba's in 1959
when Havanans first saw such exotic birds as Americans.
The first phone call I made in Lima got me a wrong number. A man with a strange accent replied anxiously,
"Please speak more slowly. I do not know Spanish very
well. I am the commercial delegate from Rumania."

At the hotel there were a correspondent from Izvestia,
a newsman from Moscow TV, the Latin American editor
of a Brazilian weekly, Sergio Pineda of the Cuban news
agency, Prensa Latina, and although in Lima the revolution visually seems not to have taken place, all conversations are political. Especially those among foreign and
local newspapermen and Peruvian intellectuals and professionals. Talking at the bar the first day, an important
Peruvian publisher came up to us and said, "You are
newspapermen, maybe you can explain it—why the verbal radicalization?" He was referring to the speeches that
President Velasco had delivered in the north during a tour
he made on the anniversary of the takeover.

Before Velasco had left, the leaders had been a little
nervous about it. True, he was going to Trujillo, the capital of the sugar cane country where the agrarian reform
had begun three months earlier, but the north has been,
since the thirties, the stronghold of the A.P.R.A. (American Popular Revolutionary Alliance), once a revolutionary, anti-imperialist party but now pro-American and
conservative though maintaining its base in the trade
unions. When the 1931 elections were fraudulently rigged
against the A.P.R.A., its followers in Trujillo revolted and
the army killed many and jailed thousands at the time. It
is ironical that the army and the A.P.R.A. have changed
roles and that the enmity continues. For A.P.R.A. leaders

it was a bitter day when the plaza at Trujillo became jammed with people hailing Velasco.

The tour of the north turned into the first popular demonstration that the military regime had gained the support of the people. "I have come here not as the head of state," Velasco declared, "but as the head of a revolution." More stringently than ever he denounced the oligarchy and the imperialists; he promised that the agrarian reform was but the first of many, and asked that old quarrels be put aside by all parties—a reference to the events of 1931 that no one ever expected an army man to make. The Aprista mayor of Trujillo made the mistake of keeping the city hall doors on the plaza closed and of not raising the flag in the president's honor. He was deposed a couple of days later, a surprising move not only because of Velasco's call for reconciliation but because, as the mayor's daring involuntarily shows, the military have not generally acted summarily against their opponents.

Obviously, Trujillo was the place to go, and I arrived there the day after the mayor lost his job, to look at the agrarian reform in operation. The public relations men of the agrarian reform headquarters met me at the airport, and it was then I met the two Soviet newsmen who were staying at my hotel in Lima and also a B.B.C. correspondent for Latin America. I did not like being tied to them to see the plantations and mills, but there was no other way. We were a disparate group: the *soveticos*, jolly and uninterested in political complexities, bent on sending home positive reports; the Englishman, reserved and elegant, wearing a vest in a town with a frontier atmosphere; all three a little puzzled at a Yankee who spoke a colloquial Spanish and with whom the Peruvians were more at home than with them.

Trujillo immediately looked like a city where a revolution had taken place. There were slogans everywhere.
Some reminiscent of Cuba's: "Elections, No; Revolution,
Yes." Some not: "Peaceful Revolution." As frequent were
the drawings of an Indian head representing Tupac
Amaru, an Indian leader who mobilized his people to
fight the Spaniards. (The slurred pronunciation of his
name has become that of the urban guerrillas of Uruguay
—*los tupamaros.*) "You know who he is?" asked one of the
PR men. "He is the symbol of our revolution." The largest
one was drawn on the sidewalk at the airport, for Velasco
to see when he stepped out of the building. A saying of
Tupac Amaru's had been appropriated by Velasco when
he announced the agrarian reform law: "Peasant, the boss
will no longer eat of your poverty."

In Lima, I had immediately heard of the two tenden-
cies within the regime—the reformists and the revolutionaries—and particular ministers and Velasco himself
were pointed out as the most Left. General Armando
Artola, the Minister of the Interior, was one of these, and
he had gone stumping in the slums of Lima, talking of the
reforms to come and promising that Peru would become
the leader of "the dispossessed countries of Latin America." A strange role for generals. They were now working
closely with intellectuals, some in the regime or in the
newspapers and weeklies that supported it, who had belonged to the Social Progresista Party, a loose coalition of
liberals and neo-Marxists who had hoped by electoral
means to accomplish the changes that the guerrillas in the
sierra wanted. It was they who were most eager to tell
you about the reforms still in the discussion stage: a banking law to put banks in the control of nationals and to
stop the flight of capital from the country; an urban re-

form to wipe out the slums ringing the city; work projects vaguely defined to create jobs.

In Trujillo, one could see a push to the Left by those heartened by the nationalization of the huge sugar plantations. The people who had hailed Velasco in the plaza had also called for amnesty for revolutionaries still in jail, and chants such as *Velasco Seguro—A los yanquis dale duro* ("Steady Velasco—Hit the Yankees hard") required only the substitution of Fidel's name for Velasco's to duplicate old Cuban ones. At the agrarian reform headquarters and in the plantations and mills there were those who felt sure that the revolution would take a more radical course than it had so far. Their rationalization took the form—as it did with left-wing newspapermen in Lima—that having decided on so radical an action as the confiscation of Standard Oil's holdings and the agrarian reform, the military rulers would be forced by the reaction of the oligarchy and the United States to take further measures to protect the revolution. It was all bound to come, they argued, and they characterized this hope with a phrase that explained for them the caution of the regime in moving so slowly: when anyone asked about a possible urban reform or wondered what the details of the banking reform, say, would be, they'd raise a finger to their lips and whisper, "Sh-h-h—don't make a racket!"—meaning that they were not going to be precipitate like the Cubans and alarm their enemies.

The administrators at the three plantations and mills we visited—two belonging to the Gildemeister family of German origin and one to the W. R. Grace Company—were, however, quite formal in their explanation of the agrarian reform there. Each was administering the business for the state until the workers in the mills and plantations were ready to run them as cooperatives. The workers had received a 10 percent increase in salaries, those due for retirement were assured that they would not lose their homes in the company towns, and workers' classes in cooperatives were being held twice daily. In one case, the cooperative would be formed no later than February, 1970; with the others the date was not certain, but later in Lima an important aide of Velasco's assured me all would be cooperatives within six months.

Since one of the sugar cane plantations was the largest in the world, I asked the administrator if turning them into cooperatives rather than state enterprises was not going to create a group of privileged workers among the impoverished population and thus cause unrest. This upset one of the Soviet newsmen sufficiently to force him to interrupt and say that he dissociated himself from the question and that he needed no such explanation, since it seemed to him that everything was going well. The administrator, however, did not mind my question and seemed, in fact, a little puzzled by the Soviet newsman's interruption. He explained that 50 percent of the cooperative's profits would go to the state and that the law stipulated that much of the remaining profits had to be set aside for improvements of the lands and mills and for investment in new industries to create jobs. Wouldn't the debt to the previous owners, to be paid over a period of twenty years, be a serious burden? The administrator was pleased to explain that the payment would be minimal and on the order of the payment on takeover; that had been about $5,000 or approximately the cost of one of the huge trucks used to haul the cane from the fields. "We figure that in any case they have made more than a reasonable profit on their investment," he added with a smile.

However deeply pleased the new administrators were to be acting against the oligarchy—a much used word in Peru—none could be called anticapitalist. Each explained that landholders throughout the country who lost their lands under the law were being encouraged to invest in new industries. The bonds they were given to mature in twenty years could be used immediately for credit if invested in a new industry within the country, so long as 50 percent of the investment consisted of new capital. They were both earnest in their explanations and neutral in the tone they adopted when speaking of the landholders in this new role, as if they could not help but have a reasonable doubt that these old oligarchs had any real interest in developing the economy of the nation. Yet the word socialism never showed up in our discussions, and cooperativism in the context of their explanations was not a euphemism for it.

At one administrator's office I glanced at a letter on his desk while he was answering the phone, and saw that he had written Lima to find out if he should continue paying foreign technicians in dollars, as their old contracts stipulated; Lima had replied that he was to hold up and they would give him final instructions soon. One of the left-wing young men with the agrarian reform administration smiled when he saw me peek at the letter. He too had peeked, and now whispered, "They will never get the dollars! Those days are over." At that mill we ate in a fine restaurant and bar used by single men working there under contract; when we left, the same young man saw me look up at a sign on the landscaped walk that led to it. It said "For Members Only," and the young man shook his head and told me, "Soon it will say, For Workers Only." The Soviet newsmen seemed not to notice any of this.

In Cartavio, W. R. Grace's former plantation and mill,

we sat in the drawing room of a beautifully proportioned mansion talking to the state administrator. It had been the living quarters of the former administrator, but the present one only had an office there. He pointed out to me that the architecture was Virginian. There was no venom in the statement; it was simply a fact he thought would interest me. I was more interested in his casual statement that the trade union of the mill workers was still headed by Apristas; he said that they had given him no trouble. "Not that they are happy," he added. "They talked agrarian reform for many years and when they had the majority in congress managed to delay and emasculate any agrarian reform law that came up."

I asked where the trade union local was, and our guide did not hesitate to take us there, though the Soviet newsmen looked pained at the prospect. The guide, however, was gleeful; it was obvious he felt I would dislike the Apristas. We found them at their headquarters, a small building in the company town, and some six officers of the local led us into the library and small meeting room of the union, where we sat around long library tables.

"Nothing has changed yet," their spokesman said when the Soviet correspondent asked them if they were pleased with the agrarian reform law. "So far all that is still in the future."

"You don't think the authorities mean what they say?" I asked.

They seemed to shrug their shoulders collectively. "We have to see."

A funny exchange along these lines continued. The Soviet correspondent worked hard to get an enthusiastic response about the new regime, but the Apristas eluded him. "But the big demonstration for President Velasco in

Trujillo showed how you felt, right?" he finally asked.
Again many shrugs, and their spokesman replied, "Well
. . . the administrator put the trucks at our disposal to go
into town, and we did not have to work that day. . . . We
had never had a president visit Trujillo . . . so we went."

There was so much disingenuousness on both sides that
I asked bluntly if their lack of enthusiasm was due to the
fact that they were Apristas and the agrarian reform was
begun by their old enemies. "Oh no, sir, we do want the
agrarian reform," one replied. "We see our job as guaran-
teeing that it will take place and to ask questions about
the law."

"Such as what?" I asked.

"Well, if someone says—as has been said—that there
will be no more trade unions, then we have to think about
that."

General Artola, the Minister of the Interior, had said in
a public speech that once the cooperatives were formed
the workers would not need trade unions, and the agrarian reform guides, who could scarcely disguise their dislike for the Apristas, began to explain Artola's statement.
Not to us but to the Apristas. Throughout our stay they
kept arguing with the trade union officers, and the trade
union officers would invariably reply, "Well, we will see."

"But even if General Artola had never made the point,"
I said, "did it not occur to you that if you truly have a
cooperative in the next few months, if the mill belongs to
you and all of you elect your administrators and set work
norms collectively, there really would be no need to have
a trade union?"

"Well . . . we shall have to see," the spokesman said.

Before we left, they again assured us of their interest in
seeing that the cooperative went through, pointed out that

they were eager to help with the classes on cooperativism, and to question details of the law to insure that a true reform went into effect. The only issue, however, that they could think of at the moment was the law's statement that at the company hospital children of employees to the age of sixteen would be treated free, whereas such a right was already in effect for children of workers dependent on their parents no matter what their age.

On the walls were framed statements in support of trade unionism. When we got up to leave, I copied one of President Eisenhower's: "Only a thoughtless person would deny workers the right to join a union of their choice." The guide nudged me and muttered, "Eisenhower!" I did not tell him that in the United States context that statement could pass as a defense of the open shop, for he was angry enough at the Apristas. "They say nothing has changed!" he exclaimed as soon as we were out of earshot. "But there is no boss in the administrator's house. Doesn't that mean something to them?"

True, the Apristas struck me as bureaucrats worried about losing their jobs (I wondered what would be the response of the Detroit U.A.W. leadership if some profoundly reformist Washington administration turned over the auto industry to the workers) but their cautiousness was something I found in most workers in the sugar mill towns we visited. No question that they supported the government. They were even glad that the mayor of Trujillo had been replaced. The class on cooperativism I attended in the middle of the day was so jammed that more than half the hundred workers squeezed into the room had no chairs to sit on, and they listened with a concentration that was quite moving. But at some point in the personal conversations I held with many there was always a moment when they refused to make any predictions about the future. "You see, sir, there have been so many promises in the past that we have to wait."

Even at Casa Grande, the largest sugar mill in the world and perhaps the most technically advanced, they live in miserable stucco attached houses. Unbroken rows line each side of the streets, in the midst of which are the latrines and faucets to supply water for the whole block. There is electricity but only wood stoves. Julio Holguin, an unskilled worker earning about $1.25 a day and living in four tiny rooms with seven children, said, "And the last time Juan Gildemeister, the old boss, was here he said we could not pick up wood or even the dried can tops to use for our fires from his fields, and you know what that means, sir." He meant that they would have to go many miles to reach the boundary of what had been Gildemeister's lands.

Yet the first thing Holguin would want the cooperative to construct is schools. Then houses. Already in the cooperativism classes you could see their interest in learning. The young teacher told them that cooperativism was brotherhood and equality, and he then reviewed the previous lesson. "In the cooperative does the member with more money have more of a say?" he asked.

"No. One man, one vote," one worker replied, and all the others laughed with delight.

"And if a leader of the cooperative uses his position to make political propaganda—for communism or the A.P.R.A.—what do you do?"

That was harder to answer. "We throw them out?" someone said.

"You vote them out," said the teacher. "There is no room for politics in the cooperative."

Something about the cooperativism teacher bothered one of the left-wing young men with us. He felt the teacher had more to learn from the workers than they from him, and a moment later when we ran into a parade of the local school celebrating its tenth anniversary, he was outraged that the band was playing the march from *The Bridge over the River Kwai.* The children wore school uniforms and carried banners showing the school was named after Juan Gildemeister. "He donated the land," a teacher explained. I asked, "Are you going to change the name?" She looked puzzled, said she thought not, and the young left-winger struck his forehead in dismay.

By the end of the long day, during which the B.B.C. correspondent had left at noon to return to Lima, I had spent some twelve hours in the company of the Soviet newsmen. I was both irritated and disgusted with them— particularly because they were citizens of a socialist country—and as I made my notes about the day and wondered, as one inevitably does, how the day's events could be incorporated into my article, I feared that my report would be less about Peru than about the failure of the Soviet Union to produce socialists. Not only because of the two newsmen. One of the young guides who had spent the day with us was a Peruvian who had studied for six years at the Patrice Lumumba University in Moscow and returned only a couple of months before the military takeover. He irked me as much as the two older men, and in much the same way.

First, much of the *sovieticos'* jolly good spirits was an admixture of boorishness and arrogance. They seldom thought of anything but their own needs and were continually interrupting others to have their say or get their needs met. We always deferred out of politeness, but once they had a disagreement because the one who was a photographer felt the other had delayed too long getting information about the method of burning the sugar cane; the screaming exchange that ensued embarrassed us all. I let them begin the formal interviews, since formal interviews do not much interest me, and they invariably began by taking out their notebooks, asking the interviewee's name and position, and spending much time getting this right. Once they got that information written down, they seemed to run out of questions, and if no one bailed them out, they asked, "Well, how is everything going?" Fine, was the reply they wanted; they could use nothing else in their reports.

I suppose I was a terrible irritant to them. They didn't quite know how to feel about me. I was good at helping them with the spelling of names, and I could think of a lot of questions to take the interviews out of the dead-ends into which they led them. They were grateful to me for that, but they could not bear the way I had of drifting away from the party and talking to people who were not officials. They felt they had to run after me and hear what I was hearing; they were always disappointed, for it was never solid information they could put in their notebooks. Not that they were indefatigable about statistics either; most of their conversation was general banter or questions about where they were going next, when we would stop to eat or turn in.

The interruption that I reported in the first interview —when one of them dissociated himself from my questions—I found to be typical. The background of my questions about the feasibility of turning such large enterprises into cooperatives had to do with the early experience of

the Cuban revolutionaries; the large cattle farms that I
had seen being built in Cuba as cooperatives were turned,
for reasons such as those I gave the Peruvian administrator, into state farms with salaried employees before they
were completed. There was nothing special about my
questions; they could be the concern of anyone, but certainly of socialists. The Soviet newsmen were always
made nervous by such a line of questioning. It occurred to
me at first that they may simply not have wanted to push
forward their own ideology, and were acting like polite
guests, but the fact was that they were apolitical, which I
imagine is the emasculated fate of all bureaucrats doing a
job.

During that first interview, I had not yet learned that
they liked to have me take over the questioning—if I did
not get into dangerous areas—and so I once stopped after
what had seemed to me was more than my due. I joked,
"But I am monopolizing the conversation, and I don't
want you to think all Yankees are monopolists." Everyone laughed, and one of the *sovieticos* turned to me with
great friendliness and said, "Like the Chinese." I should
not have been surprised; I had once lunched with a group
of Czech bureaucrats, and their jokes about the Chinese
were on the same level as the businessmen's luncheons I
had once had to attend. I was sufficiently disgusted to say
to the *sovietico*, "I do not think I agree," and for the next
few hours they decided I was a Maoist.

They were most at ease with the young guide who had
studied in Moscow. The guide had explained to me that
his method of enrolling at the Patrice Lumumba University had been to travel to Santiago de Chile and apply for
the scholarships that were being offered then to young
people of the third world. I had thought that communism

had an attraction to him, but he confessed that he was not a *político*, that it was simply the subsidized opportunity to become an agricultural engineer that had made him take the step. He spoke a perfect Russian, according to the *sovieticos*, and this was probably one of the reasons they took to him. But the fact was that he was as apolitical as they, though on the surface he was pleased about the new government, defended the Soviet Union, was opposed to the oligarchy and the imperialists.

I had talked to other young Latin Americans who had different stories about the Patrice Lumumba University. On the occasion of the death of Che, the authorities had been uninterested in the Latin Americans' desires to have commemorative meetings, had denied them the right to hold a demonstration in the city, and had expected them to take no notice of the event in any way. One told me that a professor had come up to one of them who had been in a group where they were tearfully talking and asked who this Guevara was that the students said had died. When the Soviet newsmen were not around, I would ask the guide disingenuous questions about his experiences there, and once he said with great approval, "And they did not teach us politics like people say. There was no propaganda. On the contrary, we were told that we were there to study and not to play at politics."

All three were careerists, and it would have surprised them to hear that they were elitists—they were so unconscious of their acts. One morning we spent time in a canefield that on the spur of the moment one of the *sovieticos* decided to film. While they went about their business, I walked over to a young Indian whose job it was to clean the field that the tractors and loaders had just cleared. It was hot, and he gathered that I enjoyed sugar cane juice as much as he, so he cut a stalk with his machete and handed it to me. I had managed to peel some of it with my fingers when the *sovieticos* returned with the guides and immediately became curious about the cane I was biting into. I explained, and one decided to try it. Without a word of explanation to the young Indian, he grabbed from him a stalk that the boy had just cleanly peeled with his machete, and turned away from him. He bit into it while walking toward our car, and said loudly, "Ugh, too sweet!" and threw the cane stalk into the sand. He got into the car and never looked at the young Indian, but I did. As far as the boy was concerned, that *sovietico* could have been a Yankee Imperialist.

As soon as we were back in Trujillo in the evening, I got away by myself and went for a walk, and ran into one of the sugar mill administrators leaving a restaurant with two friends. The three were middle-aged, all old friends; one was a traveling salesman, the other an owner of a group of stores specializing in feeds, fertilizers, and farm machinery. The traveling salesman was an Aprista, the businessman a typical middle-class supporter of the regime, and the administrator, now that he was away from his job and formal interviews, an admirer of revolutionary Cuba. In a moment he and the businessman were arguing violently with the Aprista.

The businessman explained that after a two-year changeover period, due to the working out of the agrarian reform, his business would do well. The old landholders were often politicians who grabbed the land, did not know how to work it, and ended up not paying their bills. The Aprista sniffed at that; he said that anyone with money was not going to invest it now, and that no small country could afford to alienate the big powers. The ad-

ministrator insisted it could be done; that is, become independent of the big powers. Who has done it? the Aprista
asked. Fidel, said the administrator.

The Aprista then unveiled an argument that even the
Maoist students I was to meet at the university in Lima
did not believe. This so-called revolution, he said, is a plot
of the C.I.A. "Listen to him," said the businessman. "We
take their oil, nationalize Grace's sugar—and he thinks it
is a plot of the C.I.A.!" I laughed, but the Aprista held
me one moment longer. He explained that all these events
so far were simply a cover for the negotiations now going
on with United States interests for the further development of the mining region. "We do not have the money to
develop it ourselves," countered the businessman. "Of
course we shall have to come to some arrangement
whereby they will make a reasonable profit." As far as
the Aprista was concerned, that proved his point.

In Lima, a fidelista newspaperman said that it was true
that the negotiations with the Southern Peru Company
were crucial—the really important part of the economy
was in the mining area, and their development was the
key to Peru's future economic health. He told me that he
had it from a rather good source that the negotiations
were tough ones: the government was asking for 80
percent of the profits. A civilian friend of Velasco's shook
his head when I repeated this to him, but he insisted that
the arrangement would have to be one that benefited
Peru; copper has been shown, he said, to be vital to developed countries, and in ten years the world's need for
it would be immeasurably greater, according to studies
done. This gave the government the upper hand in its
negotiations, and if by the end of the year no equitable
arrangement was reached, there were other developed

countries that would be pleased to meet their demands.

In the cocktail lounge of the Hotel Bolivar (its rating in Lima is comparable to the Plaza's in New York) a day later, Enrique Zilleri, editor of a weekly magazine, brought up the subject of the mines too. With his eyes he indicated where the head of southern Peru was siting in the room, and although he said no more, he obviously meant that the man's presence belied the revolutionary rhetoric of the government. Zilleri is the best known of the journalists who had had trouble with the government; he was once picked up, put on a plane to Spain, and then a couple of weeks later allowed to return. His magazine, *Caretas*, has the format of *Look*, holds to no particular political line, and with its skeptical, irreverent manner must act as something of an irritant.

"I think it is really a matter of style," is the way he explains his troubles with the regime. He believes the generals are serious men, concerned about bringing stability to the country, but he thinks the way they go about it compounds their troubles. They make an enormous hullaballoo about the oil and the plantations and are then surprised about the flight of capital from the country and the fact that most construction has come to a standstill in Lima. He feels that many of their errors—such as the expulsion of the mayor of Trujillo—are the result of the kind of impulsiveness that goes with the emotional make-up of militarists.

The psychology of the generals who made the revolution—some say it is a revolution made by the young colonels—comes up in conversations with everyone, even Marxists. Every bookstore in Lima carried Victor Villanueva's brilliant study, *A New Military Mentality in Peru?*, which traces the army's relations wth the old financial and landholding families that are supposed to compose Peru's oligarchy. But no one in Lima that I talked to seemed to know of the Rand Corporation's monograph by Luigi Einaudi published that year but completed before the coup in 1968; in it Einaudi concludes, after reviewing the Peruvian Army's history since the end of the last century and noting the sociological concerns of the curriculum of the Center for Higher Military Studies (C.A.E.M.), that its generals if they intervene in the future political life of the country will do so out of serious social motives and not out of simple personal ambition.

C.A.E.M. was established by the army at the beginning of this decade to give courses to its officers in economic, social, and political problems. Some Latin Americans enjoy telling you that it was probably set up at the recommendation of the Inter-American Defense Council—a proposition for all Latin American armies by our own Defense Department to urge on them a new role in their countries, one to counteract the epithet of "gorillas" from the left. Marxist professors were hired at C.A.E.M., young officers were sent to countries like Israel, Algeria, and Yugoslavia to study the problems of small nations, and the whole program simply backfired—they became anti-Yankee. This is a theory of which I have no personal knowledge, but it makes for a nice little irony. The fidelista newspaperman believed, as well, that the army's experiences in fighting the guerrillas in 1965 had made them open their minds to the needs of the people.

There was also the fact that in the Peruvian Army the common soldier of poor background has the opportunity —as did General Velasco, who comes of a working-class family from Piura in the north—to rise from the ranks, thus bringing into the higher echelons a social consciousness that does not exist in the elitist staffs of other Latin American armies. Part of the Peruvian officers' enmity toward the old families can be attributed to such slights as their never—or hardly ever—having been accepted in the Nacional, Lima's most exclusive social club, as Batista was never accepted into the Havana Country Club. Consequently, the army officers, by this process of separation through training from the lower middle classes and of exclusion through snobbery from the ruling families, do form a separate group. A much-reproduced photograph of General Velasco in Trujillo being hugged by a burly campesino who broke through the lines in the plaza symbolized their reaching out for support from the masses: Velasco was pleased, the photograph clearly showed, but there was a stiffness in his stance, a holding back that showed he was not comfortable with the role.

If the generals were really interested in coming closer to the people, as those who argued with me that the revolution was inevitably bound for a socialist goal said they were, there seemed to me to be a simple solution. They should form a mass political party to support their program. They also needed a newspaper to propagandize their ideals and programs, though not as much of the press fought them as they said. These were questions I decided to ask the two men who I was told were the closest to Velasco. The first one I met was Agusto Zimmerman, the civilian mentioned above, who was editor-in-chief of *El Comercio*, the most influential newspaper and also the one with the widest circulation. Zimmerman was said even to have written some of the president's speeches, and although I did not have personal knowledge of this, he so often used the pronoun "we" in his replies that he felt obliged to tell me at one point that he was not, of course, speaking for the government.

Zimmerman did not hesitate to assert that the country was, in truth, experiencing a genuine revolution, and he agreed that the regime needed its own newspaper and "means of communications." (I had reason to believe that the Miro Quesada family, which owns *El Comercio*, though traditonally anti-Standard Oil in the controversies about the legality of its holdings in Peru, reins in the enthusiasm of Zimmerman for the regime and was not allowing *El Comercio* to play the role that Zimmerman wanted.) But not a mass political party. "What we need is technicians to implement our programs," he said, as if closing a door.

Like middle-class supporters of the military, he informed me that if the revolution had not taken place, Peru would have gone socialist. The Marxists made a mistake, he believes, when they fail to distinguish between equality of opportunity for all men and the inequality of individuals. Yet in all men there is the need to aspire to more and more, and it is to this need that the revolution responds. When, as an example of the need for reforms, I mentioned the dreadful shanty towns that ring Lima, he corrected me and said that the peasants who have set themselves up there have bettered themselves and will continue to do so. "They are truly young towns, not slums."

Perhaps because he is a civilian, he argued that the 1968 coup was not a military one. No more than a handful, perhaps as little as six generals, participated in the takeover. "It is Velasco's revolution," Zimmerman said. Talking of the Plant Protection case reported cryptically in the newspapers that morning (a group of people had been arrested and documents confiscated from an American owned organization that supplied company guards to industries and was also reputed to act as a blacklister for the personnel departments of all businesses) Zimmerman volunteered a new explanation for the resignation of two generals from the cabinet in February. They, he said, had been part of a C.I.A. plot "to make a Mossadegh" of Velasco. "You may be sure that the C.I.A. is active here," was all he would say about the Plant Protection case.

Zimmerman is an educated and sophisticated man, and his anti-Americanism is, consequently, a good gauge of how much enmity we have created for ourselves in Latin America. He was only half serious when he gave as example of the commercialization of our culture a typical New Yorker deciding that the better of two classical concerts must be the one with higher-priced seats. However, there was no mistaking his feelings when he said passionately, "The United States has a superior technology, greater production, all that—but it does not have a culture, and it never will!" His inability to control that outburst stayed with me for a long time.

A thoroughly cool and equable man was Jose Matos Mar, head of the Institute of Peruvian Studies, an independent organization financed by French and American universities and private contributions. (The Maoist students in Lima see the long arm of the C.I.A. in it.) They have sponsored important studies by sociologists, anthropologists, and economists, and Matos Mar seemed a good man to ask if what was going on was a classical revolution. The question amused him no end.

"Oh no, no, this is no revolution. A modernization of the economy, yes, but no revolution. I do not mean that it is bad. On the contrary. For the first time you could say that we feel we really have our feet on the ground, that we can be proud. But it is simply a modernization, an attempt to make things work efficiently. We shall live more decently, the whole population's standard of living will rise—all that but no more. It is just a change, though a good one, within the old structure."

It is Matos Mar's contention that the revolution's success will depend on the United States, for modernizing the economy can only be done in a world context, and the United States can stop the Peruvians from buying and selling in the world market. Peru has a chance, he believes, because it is no longer raw materials that should interest the economy of the United States, but what the United States can do with them. "We are under the domination not of oil and copper but of paper clips and nylon and all those articles for consumption that we cannot make. But you know all that from your Galbraith." He feels that another development in Peru's favor in being accepted in this new role is the infectiousness of its revolution, and he cited the developments in Bolivia, Argentina, Chile, and Brazil, where militarists were showing some of the same nationalist aspirations.

However detached Matos Mar's view is of what is going on, he was spending weekends in the country with colleagues to help the Indians draw up papers, in accordance with the agrarian reform law, to set up farming cooperatives. The law means not only to eradicate large estates (*latifundios*) but also the tiny, uneconomical farms (*minifundios*) on which the Indians live on the edge of starvation. In the sierra where the Indians have been defrauded of their lands for centuries the agrarian reform law has run into trouble: the Indians see no reason to pay, even over a twenty-year period, for lands they have made cultivable and that were stolen from them.

It was on these Indians that the 1965 guerrillas counted for support, and an analysis of their failure has been written by the most important surviving guerrilla leader, Hector Bejar. He had headed the E.L.N. (Army of National Liberation) which had fought in the province of Ayacucho, not too far from where the M.I.R. (Movement of the Revolutionary Left) headed by Luis de la Puente operated. Put rather simply, the first had developed in the main from a group that had left the Communist Party (influenced by the Cuban view of the necessity for armed struggle) and the second from the A.P.R.A. (disgusted by the turn to the Right of the old revolutionary party). Both held socialism to be their eventual goal, and their immediate ones were similar: a popular front government, expulsion of all foreign monopolies, agrarian reform, and the establishment of ties with all countries of the world. They held many conversations to coordinate their guerrilla program but never came to an agreement to act as one. Their inability to do so, according to Bejar, was one of the factors in their defeat; their operations began in early 1965, and despite initial successes they were wiped out by the end of the year. De la Puente was killed in action, but Bejar was caught alive.

His book won the *Casa de las Americas* prize in Havana in January, 1969, and the Peruvian edition could be bought in any bookstore in Lima. That was not the only sign of the liberality of the regime, although it has harassed some dozen newspapermen, as in the case of Zirelli. In fact, although the government rules by decrees and appoints officials without consultation, in November of 1968 it reestablished constitutional guarantees suspended by Belaunde's administration. The generals have given new meaning to the term "benevolent dictatorship." I found it astonishing to read newspapers and magazines criticizing the government or to browse, say, through Moncloa's bookstore on Plaza San Martin, where revolutionary literature from all Latin America is prominently displayed. I was able to buy there records and books from Cuba that our government does not allow in our country.

In that same plaza, while watching a superb pantomime show by a mime who had decided to take his theater to the people, I met two young Peruvian journalists and was more than astonished to learn from them that I could visit Hector Bejar in El Sexto, a prison in the center of the city.

They looked puzzled when I asked how I could obtain permission, and I explained that other journalists at my hotel had thought it was out of the question. "Tomorrow is visiting day for political prisoners," one said. "We shall pick you up at nine." And at nine we walked to El Sexto, which occupies one square block, and pushed our way through the crowd of friends of "common" prisoners who hoped to bribe a guard and be allowed in. A guard opened the door a few inches, asked if I was visiting a political prisoner, and let me squeeze through when I nodded. There was a crush in the small room inside, but the guard behind a battered desk asked for my identification papers. He did not blink when I gave him my passport but simply gave me a metal disk with a number, as if I were checking a hat, and pointed me to a door.

Beyond the door arose the din of a hundred simultaneous conversations, and it was only at this point that I was asked, by a guard who held the door ajar for me, whom I was visiting. "Hector Bejar," I said, and he repeated the name into the mike in his other hand. I heard it boom twice over the long alleyway I stepped into; on the right was a nine-foot wall, on the left an outside wall of the enormous jail. There are fifty other political prisoners in the place, and they must all have received many visitors, for it was difficult to make my way through them. All smiled and nodded, sure that anyone visiting that day must wish them well. One of the young journalists caught up with me and took me to Bejar, who was waiting at the

end of the alleyway. He shook my hand, unsurprised, and
motioned me to perch alongside him on a ledge that stuck
out some six inches from the wall.

I could not think of any serious question to ask him; I
could only exclaim at how extraordinary the whole thing
had been. "I was only lightly frisked," I said. "I could have
brought you anything—just anything!" They smiled po-
litely, and I explained that in the summer I had visited
my stepson in a New York civil jail, a Columbia student
convicted of a contempt charge. "And there is no comparison," I said. "We talked to each other on either side of
two layers of unsynchronized wire screens—and *he* only
occupied a university building!"

Bejar enjoyed that, and when I finished describing the
bureaucratic detail of visiting a prisoner in one of our jails,
both he and the young journalist told me that the fight for
the rights of political prisoners was a long, hard-fought
one in Peru. He had been held in a modern jail in the
countryside, but he asked to be transferred to El Sexto so
that his wife could visit him more frequently. "Of course
they honored my request," he said. "This is the second
worst jail in the country." The worst is El Frontón, on an
island off the coast, where the Trotskyist Hugo Blanco, an
organizer of peasants, has been held since 1963.

Bejar is in his early thirties, looks at everyone with
clear, unguarded eyes, and has that lightness of spirit that
seems the special gift of persons totally committed to a
dangerous course of struggle. What do you think, I asked
first, of the new government. "I view it with total distrust,"
he said. "These are the people who napalmed whole vil-
lages to hunt us down."

"What do you think of the Cubans' statements about
this revolution?" I asked.

"I think they are overenthusiastic," he said.

I asked if he thought that so many years of isolation from the rest of Latin America may have made them see revolutionary developments where none exist. It was obvious he hated to talk about this. "I really cannot say," he replied. "I do not have the knowledge nor the moral authority to criticize the Cubans." He thought that over and then added, "But we have the responsibility to decide about our own country."

At that moment a double line of young men, wearing suits and ties, were led into our end of the alley. "Law students," Bejar said. An old guard lectured them before taking them to the iron-grilled door into the prison. "Now remember, gentlemen, those are not little angels you are going to see inside," he said. "So keep your hands in your pockets and your eyes wide open at all times, and be careful, careful."

A moment later, more law students, this time girls. "Oh no," said Bejar to me. "No one inside is allowed to have their wives or women come sleep with them. There is every kind of perversion. . . ." The girls came back quickly, pale and holding on hard to their composure.

Although technically the political prisoners are not supposed to receive political literature, Bejar is well informed and is writing another book. I told him I had been to Trujillo and the plantations, and he asked me to tell him about it. I said that I found every worker I spoke to supported the government and liked the agrarian reform, and I described the classes in cooperativism. He asked me what I thought of what I had seen, and I said that I thought these were changes for the better. "But paternalistically implemented," I said, "and it seemed to me that the people were accepting of this treatment, even meek."

It hurt him to hear me say this, and he put a hand on my arm and shook his head. "Our people are not meek, believe me."

"These are all bourgeois reforms," he commented a moment later. "If you can stand to read the agrarian reform law, you will see that in the sierra individuals are allowed to own quite large tracts of land." Like Matos Mar he believes that all that is occurring is a modernization of the economy, an attempt to create a larger middle class of consumers; but for him this is a bitter fact, and he will not fool himself that it has not disarmed the Left, at least temporarily.

Bejar had been in jail three years then and had yet to be tried. Since the militarists took power, there had been no change in their treatment of him and the other political prisoners, and when I told him that Zimmerman believed he should be freed and that the fidelista newspaperman assured me he would, he replied, "I do not believe it." He laughed when he explained that the judge and prosecutor assigned to his case both had relatives who had been killed in engagements with guerrillas. "So you can see why I am not hopeful."

The hour was over, and all around us people were embracing to say goodbye with an intensity that was beautiful. I asked one last question: if he got out now, would he go back to what he had been doing? He smiled. "Okay, that was a bad question," I said, but I knew from his book that he had not written it as an historical exercise but as an object lesson for those he hoped would take up the fight.

On the two days left to me in Peru—for the last I had an appointment in the Government Palace with a colonel who is supposed to be Velasco's most influential political aide—I met two women who were fighting a kind of rear-guard action for the Left. One was a woman lawyer, Laura Caller, tall, impassive, calm, at her small cramped office in the center of the city, the equally small outer office crammed with people. "Ah, you have only one more day in Peru. Too bad. You could have come with me to my part of the country—Cuzco, Ayacucho—on horseback, on foot. Seen some of my clients. You know what it is to hear an old Indian woman say to you in her language, We have to keep on fighting as Señor Mao said"? The language is Quechua, and Laura Caller speaks it too, having been brought up in Cuzco by a family of very unorthodox ways. Besides the Indians, her clients are some of the left-wing unions, political prisoners—anyone, in fact, in trouble with the government.

She has never belonged to a political party, is impatient of theorizing, and is moved only by people who are activists. She leaves home in the morning and never gets back before midnight, picking up a bite here and there during the day. Her friends worry that she is not controlling her diabetes, or that she does not collect from her clients; one saw her rush away at the moment that a client had taken out his wallet, because a messenger had arrived with the news that an activist had been jailed. "You have to get there fast or they will be tortured," she explained. "Once the lawyer gets there, they are not touched—one of the few guarantees left."

Her conversation is like a series of guerrilla thrusts, laconically delivered. "Matos Mar spends weekends helping the peasants draw up the cooperative applications? Why doesn't he give an official one hundred dollars—the papers will come through in five days." "Agrarian reform in the sierra—the Indians have made their own agrarian reform, only they are not going to pay anyone for their lands." "Peruvian writers? The things that the Indians are doing, real dramas, and what is Mario Vargas Llosa doing abroad?" "I am tired of legalism—the legalisms of the agrarian reform that works against the poor peasant, the excuses in court to prove my clients were not there or could not have committed the acts, when in fact they are proud of what they have done."

In her office was Blanca La Barrera, the kind of person Laura Caller likes, a woman in her thirties who has spent all her adult life trying to help others. She began as a Jehovah's Witness and still remembers vividly the shock of entering the hovels of the Indians among whom she was sent to preach. She has worked with almost every political party of the Left in Peru and found them wanting. "Oh Blanca, my friends say, I think you miss your old organization. And I do, I miss their wonderful organization. If revolutionaries were as well organized, the revolution would have already taken place."

In the early 1960s, she went to the sierra to join Hugo Blanco when she heard he was organizing the peasants, and she has a six-year-old boy by him. She has been jailed twice, but the charges have never stuck, and she now lives in Lima, supporting herself and her child by sewing, and spending every extra moment working for the defense committee of the Ayacucho victims. In June the students and teachers of Ayacucho, a town in the mountains south of Lima, demonstrated against the education reform law, demanding that payment for courses in which students have failed be canceled, and the government, Blanca said, gunned them down.

"The revolutionary government?" I exclaimed.

"Of course, they meet you with bullets whenever the

people make any demands," she replied, an octave higher than my exclamation, for it is astounding to her that anyone should think the military regime is anything but oppressive.

The education reform law is not popular. It abolished student government and political organizations in the colleges, and in the secondary schools, as the Ayacucho people protested, it required students to pay almost one dollar a month for each course they were repeating. That is an enormous sum for poor people in Peru, and the requirement has since been abolished. But many people were wounded, some killed, and forty-six were arrested. "There are still seven in El Sexto," Blanca said. Among those arrested in Ayacucho was a lawyer who worked for the peasants' organization in nearby Huanta, and the Indians there, who are very loyal to persons who help them but distrustful of anyone else, as Blanca put it, came into Huanta determined to free him from jail. They too were fired on, and the Ayacucho committee can only estimate the number killed. Some one hundred—"and perhaps more, because the wounded flee," Blanca said, "in order not to be arrested, and they may have died in the fields."

I must have looked incredulous, for Blanca said, "You find it hard to believe? But that is the way our people have always lived." She sighed and gathered up her papers. "Is it any wonder that the Indians hate and distrust the *misti* [the white man] or that they say of the agrarian reform *la ley engaña cholos*—the law deceives the Indians?"

The Government Palace takes an entire block of the Plaza de Armas in the old city, a stunning square whose colonial buildings encrusted with enclosed balconies of hand-carved hardwood are perfectly preserved because it

never rains in Lima. Behind the iron-grilled fence and
gates of the palace the guards, like tropical birds in their
black and red uniforms topped by silver and brass helmets
with red plumes, go through a goose-stepping ritual when
relieved twice each day. Three stand as sentinels at the
side door, a rifle at the shoulder, a dagger at the hip, and
it was a surprise they could speak and refer me to a large
anteroom where two male secretaries asked my business. I
had an appointment with Colonel Leonidas Rodriguez,
the most influential political aide of the president, according to those who believe that Velasco was a figurehead for
the young, nationalist colonels.

He was two hours late, but when my time came I exchanged my passport for a tag to be pinned to my lapel,
and was led by a functionary across long foyers whose pat-
terned floors were worked with marble of various colors,
up stairways, down broad halls, to the anteroom of Colonel Rodriguez's office. It gave onto an Andalucian patio,
tiled with superb *azulejos*, in which a small fountain
played. Men emerged from it carrying silver centerpieces
filled with sprays of red roses. A secretary invited me to
cross the patio and enter a long eighteenth-century
French drawing room whose Aubusson rugs and gilt furni-
ture was as fresh as the roses. Colonel Rodriguez entered
from the opposite end, wearing his uniform, but all ease
and informality. He was astounded that I had waited so
long; he had hoped his office would have put me off when
he was called by the president—and he immediately ordered coffee for us. It was served in gold-edged Limoges.

I asked him, to begin with, if he considered this a revolution in the classical sense. Echoing Velasco, he said that
the revolution had only begun three months ago, with the
agrarian reform. He answered so fulsomely, going into an

explanation of the grip of the oligarchy on all life in Peru, that I feared it would be difficult to guide him in the direction I wanted. To explain the consciousness that had finally led them to take power, he told me an account of a deer hunt he attended in Ecuador when he was military attaché there.

"A friend of mine, a man whom you could say belonged to the oligarchy there, invited me for a weekend to his country estate, knowing how much I like to shoot deer. A magnificent place, miles of beautiful wilderness. In the morning, when we gathered to mount our horses, I carried my spurs in my hands and was about to put them on when a peasant threw himself on the ground and said, *Patron*, do not bend down—I shall put them on for you."

Colonel Rodriguez shook his head. "For a man to shine shoes is one thing, he earns his lving that way. But to have men bred so servile . . ." He looked at me to see if I understood. "That is why we say about our revolution that our theater of operations, to use a military term, is man."

I told him about the Rand Corporation report on the army, and I asked him if they had prepared to take power. "We did not have the slightest intention. The studies were simply to understand our country better." In 1965 the army waited until President Belaunde gave them the job of suppressing the guerrillas—they did not move until then, he said—and they were able to finish them off in six months because they knew exactly where to find them. "But when we finished the job, we gave Belaunde a report that in effect said, the guerrillas are suppressed but now it is up to you to consolidate the victory—the problems still remain, and they cannot be solved by military operations."

I asked him if there was any truth to the view that the

army officers learned a great deal from the Marxist professors in C.A.E.M. and that fighting the guerrillas had also taught them some of the ideals of those men. He did not think that their study of Marxism had done anything more than teach them what it was, to understand it better. "About the guerrillas, I guess we did learn something from them—though perhaps it was the whole process itself that we gained from." He paused a moment and paid a tribute to the guerrilla fighters. "These men who gave up material well being for their ideals—even their lives—must be respected."

"Are you going to free them?" I asked quickly.

The question made him frown. "I could not say," he replied, and looked away as if to indicate that I had exceeded the proper bounds of an interview.

He did not agree with Zimmerman's view that the revolution was Velasco's and not the military's. "President Velasco himself rejects the slightest suggestion of *caudillismo*," he said. But he enjoyed Zimmerman's use of an old Spanish saying to explain why the regime always sprang its laws as a surprise: *Guerra avisada no mata moros,* which translates as "A war that has been announced will not kill any Moors." He explained the negotiations going on with the Southern Peru Company as had all supporters of the regime: "We are now exploring ways of coming to an agreement that will be attractive to us both."

I had heard rumors that negotiations were going on also with the fishing industry (Peru is one of the important producers of fish meal) which is mostly American owned. As part of their attempt to control the movement of capital, the leaders were demanding that all exportation by the fishing industry be in the hands of the government.

He seemed surprised I knew that much, but smiled and said, "There are talks, and that is one possibility being discussed."

I asked him if their present difficulties were not almost insuperable—the illegal flight of capital was supposed to have reached one hundred million this year, unemployment was on the increase, there was no new private investment nor expansion, representatives of creditor nations were at that moment meeting in Lima to renegotiate old loans. "We knew we were going to find such problems when we took power but it did not hold us back. We are having to deal with them and that is why we are contemplating so many other reforms. We expect that the people will understand."

Hadn't they thought of forming a mass political party to support the revolution? He shook his head. I told him I had been at the university and listened to what the students had to say about the education reform law. "The law does not operate—the students defy it," I said, "by their organizations and protests. Don't you think it has been a great mistake?"

"I do!" he said and burst into laughter when he saw how surprised I was. "Yes, it was a mistake. We thought we were going to encourage them to devote themselves to their studies, to preparing themselves to help the nation, for we need them—but—" And he threw out his hands and got up. He had to leave—it was now the fourth time a messenger had come to inform him that a meeting was awaiting his presence—but he did not hurry. "We shall have to do something about it," he added, and he apologized again for having made me wait. He made a turn toward the patio, as if willing to escort me, but I said I knew my way out.

My footsteps rang in the marble halls; at one turn of a graceful staircase I looked down on the sergeant of the guards—he wore gold epaulets and carried a sword—inspecting a lowly guard: the black shining boots, the plumes, the horse's mane falling down the back of the helmet, the whole absurd uniform was in order. The revolution had not changed that. It struck me that along with the emotional impulsiveness of militarists who delight in surprises, they were also deliberate and assured. No one could hurry them; not the United States State Department, the left-wingers who supported them, nor the mass of people who were in the main hungry and deprived.

Afterword

In Lima I used to have all the morning papers delivered with breakfast to my room, and as soon as I finished leafing through them I would run off to my first appointment. One morning, on reaching the lobby, I discovered I had left a crucial address in my room, and I took the elevator up again in a hurry—in so much of a hurry that I forgot to pick up my room key at the desk, something that did not occur to me until I turned into the long hall leading to my room. The linen cart, however, stood in front of it, the door was open, and I quickened my pace so as not to have to ask the chambermen to unlock it again. I thus turned into the room quickly and surprised the two young men—they were squatted before my breakfast tray, one drinking the milk for the coffee, the other biting into a cold piece of toast. I cannot remember how we got through the next ten seconds. What remains with me is the frozen image of their upturned faces reflecting shame and fear.

I cannot shake this incident off because at its heart there is the reminder that I could not put the young men at their ease. No matter what I tell myself, I am someone of whom they must be wary. For me this is not simply the dilemma of a liberal tourist in a hungry country; I tend to elevate such an incident into a symbol of what our relations, as Americans, are to South Americans. I am reminded of the Englishman and Indian in E. M. Forster's *A Passage to India*. They are men whose sensibilities create many affinities; the two should make ideal friends and yet they cannot be. On the novel's last page, the Indian rebuffs the other. "Not yet," he says, and does not need to explain, because the Englishman understands that first the crime of imperial domination must be wiped out.

After I finished this book, I took a week off to attend a conference in New York on "The Intellectual and Political Power in the Americas" and to speak at a New England college and at a conference on Latin America held at Harvard by the Boston World Affairs Council. It seemed to me that all these activities were proof that there is, as I said earlier, great interest in Latin America now. Even disinterested interest. At the first gathering the participants were Latin Americans and Latin Americanists, all experts in their fields, and two or three were social scientists with no particular knowledge of Latin America. Some of the Latin Americans worried that others were methodologists and

that the discussion might never get down to the specifics
of their continent's situation, but the three-day discussion
proved their fears wrong. The methodologists engaged in
their abstractions, but the Marxists also got their say. It
was not surprising that the group came to no conclusion
to which all could subscribe—they were all well formed
or, in any case, well hardened intellectually and ideologi-
cally—but Cuba and the revolutionary movements of the
last five years were never analyzed or considered. In three
days of talk Che Guevara was not named, and he is, I
think, the Latin American intellectual of recent times
most overtly concerned with political power.

Students and Boston liberals are different. They are
eager for information and eager to try out their theories of
what the Latin American reality is and what is wrong or
right about our actions there. What one says to them
seems, consequently, to have value. In the give and take
of such discussions a wonderful energy is generated, one
that creates an aura of good will in which the ideal solution for this worst of all worlds appears feasible and possible. El Dorado shimmers on the horizon, and everyone is
tempted to ask the ultimate questions. There came that
moment in Boston—I was member of a panel debating,
with many interjections from the audience, how we can
best establish channels of communications with Latin
American radicals—when the most interested wanted to
know what we could do to help Latin America. It was the
end of a day-long conference, and this question seemed
necessary to give it point. Everyone wanted it answered.

Away from the ambience of such a discussion, any answer looks easy, even self-indulgent. Powerless intellectuals
must shy away from them. Whatever your reply you can't
not avoid pomposity and self-importance. But I suc-

cumbed, and I must tell you what I said. I discovered
that a sentiment I lightly mentioned—and then only in
passing—in the first chapter of this book, while discussing
the Rockefeller Report, was my most felt conclusion: we
must turn our backs on Latin America and let it work out
its own destiny. It sounded like arid advice, I'm sure, to
that audience so full of sympathy and good will, especially
since the effort to convince our rulers of this would be better directed toward establishing a government that in its
relations with South America would not be motivated by
the coarsest of self-interest. Thinking about it now, I still
would not withdraw my statement; short of a revolution
in our country, the negative advice is more practicable: it
would draw support not only from that concerned audience but also from people of ill will. *Yeah, let them
make it on their own,* I can hear my compatriots say. Let
them, I say; the Cubans did.

In the audience there was a sizable group of Latin
Americans, graduate students in the main, and what I
said was echoed when they spoke from the floor. I should
not say "echoed," for it was obvious to me that however
much that comment and others of mine pleased them,
they did not want me to be the one to say any of them,
just as the blacks do not want white liberals to speak for
them. One Chilean, in fact, got up to take issue with me;
he did not think the M.I.R. in his country was as important as I said, he believed the United States would no
longer intervene militarily in South America, and he
ended, as if he were still disagreeing with me, with the
plea that we leave them alone. There was no answering
him.

As a people and as individuals we cannot be one with
them. Not yet. But there is always a human residue; I can-

not forget them. I had planned in this afterword to re-
count, as Victorian writers did in the last chapter of their
novels, what became of some of the people I met down
there. It would be a tease: many cannot write me—nor
could I reply without endangering them—and there is no
predicting what the lives of any are like this moment. One
piece of news from Brazil I cannot forget; Harry Jenkins
sent it to me in a roundabout way. It was a clipping from
a local newspaper, meant to remind me of one of the people whom he had been responsible for my meeting. The
clipping contained a photograph of a lovely girl, more
mature apparently than any of the ones from the College
of Social Sciences whom Jenkins' daughter had brought to
see me; and Jenkins must have thought of that and also
of the fact that I had not been given the names of any.
He identified her for me by writing on the margin, carefully translating my name and quoting from my article:
"Joe Church's 'sweet girl of nineteen.'"

I looked at her photograph a long time, and I remembered the recital she had given me, as spokesman for the
group, of the horrors she expected me to report, and the
shy way in which she asked for a contribution for the students who, like her, had to stay away from home those
days. The clipping now informed me that she was a
"wanted criminal," wanted for assaulting a bank. Which
one of us would not help save that darling girl? But can
we?

Jose Yglesias
North Brooklin, Maine
June 1970

ABOUT THE AUTHOR

Jose Yglesias was born in 1919 in Tampa, Florida, of Spanish-Cuban parents. He left home two days after graduating from high school, spent three years in the Navy during World War II, and eventually settled in Manhattan. He has published two novels, one nonfiction book on Cuba, and a "personal narrative" about a trip to Galicia, Spain. His articles, reviews, and stories have appeared in *The New Yorker, Holiday, The New Republic, The Nation,* and *The New York Times Magazine.* Mr. Yglesias presently lives in Maine with his wife, Helen, and their three children.